Rehearsing the Soul

52 Devotions for the Church Choir

Terry W. York

Abingdon Press
Nashville

Rehearsing the Soul:
52 Devotions for the Church Choir

This book is printed on acid-free, recycled paper.

ISBN 0-687-09849-1

Scripture quotations, unless otherwise noted, are from the New Revised Standard Version Bible, copyright © 1989 by the Division of Christian Education of the National Council of the Churches of Christ in the USA.

05 06 07 08—10 9 8 7 6 5 4 3

MANUFACTURED IN THE UNITED STATES OF AMERICA

Preface

It is the choir's responsibility to sing expressions of faith, testimony, prayer, and praise that are beyond the music of the congregation. Upon hearing the choir sing, the worshiper should feel an enthusiastic and satisfied "Yes" deep in his or her soul. "Yes, that is what I wanted to say and I adopt it as my expression as well."

For this to happen, the choir must prepare in three ways. The most obvious of the three is musical preparation. Ill-prepared music will be a distraction, even to nonmusical members of the congregation. The choir must do its best to prepare the musical vehicle that will carry the message of the text.

Second, the choir must establish a warm rapport with the congregation. The connection must happen corporately as the congregation develops a deep sense of trust in the choir and a high expectation level for the choir. The congregation must be able to trust the choir to sing music to which they can relate. Further, the congregation has a right to expect the choir to represent them knowledgeably as they sing the songs the congregation cannot sing.

It becomes important, then, for members of the choir to accept the personal and individual responsibility to connect with congregants outside the choir loft in the context of the broader life and work of the church. If the choir is to sing prayers and praise on behalf of the congregation, they must be a part of the congregation. The choir and congregation should experience the church's joys and struggles together.

Third, the choir must prepare spiritually. The choir member would do well to approach his or her presentation of scripture and spiritual truth with the same sense of awe and dependence on the Holy Spirit as that of the minister who will deliver the sermon. God's message, whether sung or spoken, remains God's message. It is important for the choir to rehearse the soul as well as the music. Pray for a personal understanding and application of the message of Sunday's anthem. In your own quiet time, read and meditate on the scripture that serves as the basis of the text of Sunday's anthem.

Still another way to prepare spiritually for the presentation of Sunday's anthem is to share times of devotional focus as a choir. That is the purpose of this book.

Go now into your rehearsals and worship leadership with an understanding of your responsibilities musically, textually, socially, and spiritually. Singing in a choir is enjoyable and enriching. In the context of a worship experience, it is humbling.

Terry W. York
Truett Seminary, Baylor University, Waco, Texas

Spring

Scripture: "But the Lord stood by me and gave me strength, so that through me the message might be fully proclaimed" (2 Tim. 4:17a).

Are Christians the world's most devoted historians or are we, indeed, disciples of a living Master? The answer can be found in part in how we, as individuals and as a choir, approach worship. If we are disciples of a living Lord, let us worship with all our heart and mind and soul. As disciples, we will be deeply and strangely aware that the unseen but very much alive Christ is present, standing beside us as we dare to worship and lead in worship. Somehow, the messages of our hymns and our anthems will get a new and closer scrutiny before they leave our souls to become words we utter in song. In the words we read, the thoughts we ponder, and the music we sing, we must ask ourselves: "Will this sound like a lie or an honest prayer to the One who stands beside me? Does my life and my intentions match what I'm singing?"

In such a time of awareness and evaluation, we realize that the anthems we are preparing in rehearsal speak first to our hearts and lives. The prayers are ours first. The praise comes from our lips first. The testimony is ours before it is the congregation's. Our role, then, as worship leaders takes on a new and personal aspect. Our preparation becomes private as well as corporate; spiritual as well as musical.

Something is blossoming in our hearts and in our understanding of our role as choir members. Spring arrives: a time when dormant life bursts forth in brilliant bloom; a time when dead things wake up to green and vibrant life. That can happen in our own souls and in our own approach to the deadening routine of midweek rehearsals and Sunday presentations. The rich soil of our souls is cultivated and stirred by the presence of the living Christ. Our songs, then, move up through the depths of our being and leap into the light. Spring and song and worship and the presence of Christ are all rehearsed here, and all experienced first here!

Prayer: "Dear God, help us to be always aware of your presence with us. May it affect how we live. Today we pray specifically, that your presence will affect how we rehearse. In Jesus' name. Amen."

Week 2

Scripture: *"Beloved, I do not consider that I have made it my own; but this one thing I do: forgetting what lies behind and straining forward to what lies ahead, I press on toward the goal for the prize of the heavenly call of God in Christ Jesus" (Phil. 3:13-14).*

Press on. I love that phrase. It says that whatever has happened in the past, however good or bad, today is more important. Today is its own day. Press on. It speaks of forgiveness and encouragement. It speaks of springlike freshness and new growth. Press on. If a backward glance reveals cold, dark failure or bright, warm success, "press on" looks forward. The congregation should be encouraged in an hour of worship to listen for the voice of God, because God knows us and in our hearts God still whispers: "Press on." The choir can give the congregation that encouragement once the choir has believed it for themselves.

Neither the choir nor any one of its members should be defined by past failures or successes. No choir wants to be known for its flaws and failures. But it is not the primary focus of a church choir to be known for its perfection and success, either. A choir rehearses in an effort to press on toward the unencumbered, effective presentation of a truth via choral music. That's something to strive for, something to be known for: presenting the truth of the gospel in a beautiful, believable, and engaging manner. That's a worthy goal for the individual Christian life as well: living the gospel in a beautiful, believable, and engaging manner. The choir is always a collection of individuals. The choir's effectiveness comes from those individuals giving themselves to a common goal as interpreted by the conductor. To "press on toward the goal for the prize of the heavenly call of God in Christ Jesus" and to express that pressing on in music is a goal well worth unusual devotion.

Work hard in rehearsal. Make the truth of the message yours and then deliver it on the wings of the most beautiful music you can produce. Perhaps you will give each member of the congregation a truth to hum or whistle during the week into which they must press on.

Prayer: "Dear God, thank you for your precious gift of forgiveness. Thank you also for the gifts of purpose and strength that help us press on into life. Help us to be aware of these gifts each day. In Jesus' name. Amen."

Week 3

Scripture: "Let your adornment be the inner self with the lasting beauty of a gentle and quiet spirit, which is very precious in God's sight" (1 Pet. 3:4).

On Sunday you will stand before or up and behind a congregation full of people who will look beautiful. Cleaned up and combed, they will be in their new spring finery. They will look like the very best that the human race has to offer. Do not be fooled. What you will be able to see from the choir loft will hide a vast array of inner bruises, cuts, and battered injuries of every emotional and spiritual kind. Let your soul sing to those souls. Seek to connect with the inner reality. Don't be distracted by the outer appearance.

We serve and praise a God who can and does make things beautiful. Certainly, to see Christ in another human being is to see beauty. Sing God's truth in the beauty of holiness and you will minister to souls in a way that may start them on a journey to inner beauty that matches their outer adornment. The Holy Spirit can bring healing and peace to those souls. Your music may well be the wings of the Spirit.

Look deep into the faces of those in need. Look deep into the eyes of the orphans, widows, and widowers, the hungry and hurting. Look deep into their faces, for there you will see the reflection of who they really are. It may well be that there you will see the reflection of who *you* really are. And it may well be that there you will also see the face of Jesus. But pause for a moment and see the congregation as a mirror. Is it not equally true that the congregation is looking at a choir of beautiful people? Robed or not, the choir is also cleaned up and combed. In tonight's rehearsal, allow the message of the anthems to clean and refresh the soul. If a healing message is to be heard by the congregation, its truth will be enhanced by a choir whose souls are also engaged in the healing process. Focus on adorning your "inner self with the lasting beauty of a gentle and quiet spirit." The whole worship experience will then become "very precious in God's sight." That's good, because this whole thing is about worshiping God, who seeks those who worship in spirit and in truth. The inner self is not as clean and healthy as the outward appearance, but it can be.

Prayer: "Dear God, create in us a clean heart so that we might lead the congregation in a healing experience of worshiping you. Take these notes and words and launch them from souls that exhibit the lasting beauty of a gentle and quiet spirit. In Jesus' name. Amen."

Week 4

Scripture: *"Again I saw that under the sun the race is not to the swift, nor the battle to the strong, nor bread to the wise, nor riches to the intelligent, nor favor to the skillful; but time and chance happen to them all"* (Eccles. 9:11).

Sometimes it seems that the writer of Ecclesiastes had a family, a schedule, and responsibilities just like ours. No one runs faster than I do. No one works harder than I do. There are some people smarter than I am, but I'm not the dumbest person on earth. It takes some intelligence to manage our home and budget and schedule. But whose hot water heater is going to croak and who is going to win the lottery seems pretty much up to time and chance. Whose kids will be doctors and lawyers, and whose kids will need doctors and lawyers is up for grabs, no matter how good a parent you are. Any one of us could have written the book of Ecclesiastes.

We are all familiar with these phrases or thoughts: My calendar is crazy. My schedule is ridiculous. My life is out of control. Perhaps the truth for some is that life is dull and boring and going nowhere. For them, having to get kids to soccer, go to the grocery store, and pick up the dog at the vet—all in forty-five minutes—sounds rather exciting.

In the music to be rehearsed tonight and this spring, watch for signs that God may have a plan and a pace for our lives. We need to know that and so do the busy people who will sit in the pews for a bit of a "breather" Sunday morning. Perhaps the music we will sing in worship will lead the worshipers to seek God's face and God's pace. Perhaps they will be able to discern God's orderliness in their lives and distill a drop or two of peace from the worship experience. Tonight is our time to find and rehearse that orderliness and peace.

Take a moment, settle your mind, and center your thoughts and your soul. Ask the Lord to help you rehearse peace. Let this prayer sink deep into your soul on its way to God.

Prayer: "Dear God, I have raced through an entire day and haven't even given you so much as a thought. Forgive me. Please help me be aware of your presence so that no matter what happens tonight and tomorrow, the path will seem straight and smooth and will be full of joy. In Jesus' name. Amen."

Week 5

Scripture: *"When Jesus came to the place, he looked up and said to him, 'Zacchaeus, hurry and come down; for I must stay at your house today.' So he hurried down and was happy to welcome him" (Luke 19:5-6).*

We are not unlike Zacchaeus. When Jesus calls us, he often has to say "Come down." We may be prone to envision ourselves as having greater solo capabilities than are actually there. Jesus calls us to come down and join the ensemble. We may find ourselves, as choir members, getting more and more into a style of music that speaks to us as musicians. When that happens it is easy to forget our responsibility to speak a musical language that the congregation can claim as their own expression to God.

Perhaps the call that is most often directed to us is to submit our talents and taste to the selections and interpretations of the conductor. That's really "coming down." Yet, like Zacchaeus, coming down at Jesus' request always results in nourishing meals with peace and restoration for dessert. Choir is a wonderful environment for rehearsing the "coming down" that is often needed in our lives and attitudes. Jesus couldn't go home with Zacchaeus until Zac came down. Perhaps that's why the action that gets the choir's good work started is called the "downbeat." Perhaps that's why a right attitude and relationship with Jesus and with the congregation feel so much like home.

Secretly we wish Jesus would come up to the level of our attitude, our experience, our taste, our talent. We wish he would come up and see if enough good work could be accomplished up there. But he doesn't. He calls to us to come down to his attitude, his vantage point. He doesn't call us to sloppy work. He doesn't call us to less than our best effort. On the contrary, he calls us to the fullness that he sees in us. But first, we must come down. Hurry and be happy to welcome him.

But what about educating the congregation? Do it. Teach them how to humble their haughty, self-sufficient spirits. Show them how to have Jesus follow them home.

Prayer: "Dear God, thank you for the talent to sing. Thank you for giving us something to sing about. Help us, in a spirit of thankfulness, to let your spirit shine and sing through us as we live our lives and lead in worship. In Jesus' name. Amen."

Week 6

Scripture: "And while they were sailing he fell asleep. A windstorm swept down on the lake, and the boat was filling with water, and they were in danger. They went to him and woke him up, shouting, 'Master, Master, we are perishing!' And he woke up and rebuked the wind and the raging waves; they ceased, and there was a calm" (Luke 8:23-24).

For some, there is a sea of sadness. This applies to Sunday's congregation and to tonight's choir. Waves of anger crash across that sea. For others, there is a sea of confusion. Waves of frustration crash across that sea. The hymnwriter William Whiting offers this prayer for storm-tossed travelers:

> Eternal Father, strong to save,
> whose arm does bind the restless wave,
> who bids the mighty ocean deep
> its own appointed limits keep;
> O hear us when we cry to Thee
> for those in peril on the sea.

On Sunday you will lead your congregation to worship the One who can calm their raging seas. Your anthem for Sunday, whatever it is, may well be heard by someone in the congregation as their cry to the "Eternal Father," whom they need to be "strong to save." Indeed, God the Creator did send God the Son in answer to the cry. Jesus is present and calm in any storm. Sing the alarm for the congregation and wonderful ministry will be a by-product of God-centered worship. For even to cry out to God to calm your storm is to acknowledge God's sovereignty.

The scripture teaches that Jehovah never sleeps. But Jesus surely did. Jesus, fully God, was also fully human and humans need rest. Jesus experienced sadness and frustration. Jesus even experienced the human emotion of fear. Hear his prayer in the garden of Gethsemane. A mere windstorm, even at sea, wasn't enough to wake the one who was worn out from battling spiritual storms. His words calmed the weather. His death and resurrection calmed all spiritual storms. Sing him awake for those in the congregation who think he is asleep and doesn't care.

And how about those in this rehearsal? Does anyone need to worship by crying out in the middle of his or her storm? Let's rehearse for Sunday by crying out in prayer and then crying out in song.

Prayer: "Creator of the wind and sea, calm our private storms. Through your Holy Spirit, speak peace into our souls. May we be awakened to the presence of Jesus in our lives and then sleep more deeply than ever before. In Jesus' name. Amen."

Week 7

Scripture: "The steadfast love of the LORD never ceases, his mercies never come to an end; they are new every morning; great is your faithfulness. 'The LORD is my portion,' says my soul, 'therefore I will hope in him' "(Lam. 3:22-24).

In his popular gospel hymn, "Great Is Thy Faithfulness," Thomas O. Chisholm includes this encouraging statement: "strength for today and bright hope for tomorrow." That should bolster every choir director and every choir member. Allow a paraphrase: strength for the rehearsal and bright hope for the performance. That paraphrase has obvious application for the work of the choir, but it also has application potential for life itself.

Each day of life, each decision made, is, in fact, the living (performance) of life. Yet, it is also rehearsal for tomorrow. We call that "experience." Experience helps us do a better job, but it comes from having done the same or similar job at least once before. Another word becomes significant when the Christian thinks about strength for today and bright hope for tomorrow. That word is *forgiveness*. We need not retreat to inactivity for fear of messing up. There is forgiveness. Forgiveness and its driving force, love, give us strength and hope.

If a choir never performed until it was absolutely assured of a perfect performance, the gospel would never be sung. Mistakes are inevitable. Occasionally, every singer is a little flat or sharp. We try to gain enough experience with a piece of music (rehearsal) to reduce the number of mistakes, but even what we call a great performance could have been better. Love motivates us to forgive the last performance and rehearse for the next one—our love for Christ, for the music, and for the challenge offered to us. In the cycle of rehearsing and performing, the gospel is sung and lived. In that cycle we find strength for today and bright hope for tomorrow. It is a type of conscious breathing: purposeful and timed inhaling and exhaling. It can and should be rehearsed.

God's love gives us the gift of purpose for rehearsal, forgiveness for performance, and a continuous second chance at the cycle. We hope to get better at it. But we will not reach perfection in this life. We give God the gift of devotion as we keep trying to offer our best.

Prayer: As your prayer, read or sing the hymn, "Great Is Thy Faithfulness."

Week 8

Scripture: *"But the hour is coming, and is now here, when the true worshipers will worship the Father in spirit and truth, for the Father seeks such as these to worship him. God is spirit, and those who worship him must worship in spirit and truth" (John 4:23-24).*

They fluttered down like leaves in autumn. But they soon stretched heavenward like the fresh green shoots of spring. They were prayer requests written on small pieces of paper, dropped from the balcony. These joined the prayer requests written by the people on the main floor. All these were passed to the pulpit area of the Central Baptist Church in Moscow, Russia. It was a moving experience: not the movement of the paper, but the movement of the Spirit. Watch for it to happen here in rehearsal and again, Sunday morning. The hour is coming (Sunday) and is now here (tonight's rehearsal), when true worshipers will worship in spirit and truth.

The rehearsal of anthems suitable for worship becomes the act of worship as each anthem is internalized. The presence of God's Spirit is experienced when people are focusing on God's truth; in rehearsal as well as in performance. Choir rehearsal becomes an entirely different experience when the choir member watches for evidence of the Spirit speaking through the music. One could argue that an anthem isn't ready until the Spirit uses it to speak to the choir.

Every Sunday since that experience in the church in Moscow, I remember seeing the little pieces of paper floating down under the weight of the expectations of the worshipers. Those expectations moved toward the front of the church in wave after wave during the service.

The responsibility of the choir to be worshipers and then worship leaders is as relentless as the waves of the ocean. Rehearse, worship. Rehearse, worship. Close your eyes and the words sound like the surf. Rehearse, worship. Rehearse, worship.

Find the responsibility and the Spirit's presence refreshing. Our Savior often ministered within the sound of the surf. Allow the personal concerns and struggles that have you near the edge to be erased by the waves, like footprints on the ocean's edge.

Prayer: "Dear God, let your Spirit fall on me here and now and rise up in me. I ask for your peace and your cleansing. Sing through me, I pray, in Jesus' name. Amen."

Week 9 **Hymn:** *"When I Survey the Wondrous Cross,"* stanza 4: *"Love so amazing, so divine, demands my soul, my life, my all," words by Isaac Watts.*

Perhaps nothing is as destructive as a divided heart; one person trying to live two lives. The Lord told us that one person cannot serve two masters (Matt. 6:24). But sometimes we are slow learners. Choir is a good place to learn the lesson of serving only one master. If the conductor is trying to be master and the organist is trying to be master, the poor choir member doesn't have a chance. I suppose if you have an organist choirmaster, you dodge one of the bullets.

One of the truths or lessons packed into Isaac Watts's magnificent hymn is that Jesus' sacrifice on the cross calls for a response of total devotion and dedication. If the love of God as seen in Jesus on the cross demands of us our soul, our lives, our all, there is little left over to give to anyone or anything else. Yet, a loving, total dedication to the Lord overflows to the benefit of the people and responsibilities that we encounter. That includes family, friends, and other choir members. It is true that other choir members and the ministry of the choir will benefit from our individual devotion, dedication, and singular focus on responding to God's "love so amazing." But that is extra. The focus of love of this magnitude is God; in this case, God the Son.

Being of a single, focused mind doesn't mean having a narrow vision. It means approaching life with purpose and interpreting life with help from God. Such focused people are rare. They usually end up being leaders. They certainly are strong contributors to the Kingdom work. They make good choir members, too. Focus on rehearsal and much more is accomplished. Focus on the text of the anthems and the soul is involved. With mind and soul engaged and focused it is easier to commit one's soul, life, and all.

The hymn's text is inspired by a vision of the cross. That's a good and proper place for the Christ-follower to focus. It is the first step in the depth of devotion that we are considering.

Prayer: "Dear God, give us singleness of heart."

Week 10

Maybe this is the year. Maybe this Palm Sunday Jesus will show up on a horse. Horses are stronger and more aggressive; horses are faster and more elegant. Maybe this year he'll ride in on a horse. My sisters and brothers, hold your horses! Again this year, in Sunday's hour of worship, the Master, our model, will ride in on a donkey. Parts of this scene are so obvious: Jesus' triumphal entry on a beast of burden rather than on one of conquest, unassuming rather than imposing, gentle rather than aggressive. Yet, there are other aspects of this scene that have even deeper impact because their message is subtler.

How difficult was it for the crowds to hail Jesus as King? Were they ridiculed by nonbelievers who were laughing at the sight of a grown man on a donkey colt? If his feet were dragging the ground, why didn't he just walk? That would have been impressive, a determined walk into the teeth of danger. No one would have laughed at that.

"Hosanna, blessed is he that comes in the name of the Lord" is a strong statement to make. Make it from the side of a dusty road or from a choir loft, it is one's belief, hope, and commitment wrapped up in just a few words. Look stronger, Jesus; I'm betting my life on you. Look more successful, Jesus; nonbelievers are watching.

What was so triumphant about the triumphant entry? Not the cheers of the crowd, which soon changed to cries of "Crucify him!" The triumph was in the fact that Jesus and his message made it to this point unchanged, undiluted, unswerving. Jesus' ministry, lifestyle, and message started out simple and humble and stayed that way in spite of every temptation, frustration, and misinterpretation. Jesus the man did not get in the way of the ministry of Jesus the Son of God. Triumph!

Sunday, you too can sing from a heart and life that made it one more time through the week and to worship. Grace and forgiveness will have kept you in the saddle, even if it was on a donkey. Sing in triumph!

Prayer: "Dear God, in your Son we have seen our model for humility and obedience. May the vision of Jesus on a donkey help us keep our lives and goals in perspective. In Jesus' name. Amen."

Week 11

Scripture: *"Mary Magdalene went and announced to the disciples, 'I have seen the Lord' "* *(John 20:18a).*

You have also seen the Lord! It is probably not any easier to tell people today that you have seen the Lord than it was three days after he had been executed. But it's just as true now as it was then. You have seen the Lord in your experiences and in the lives of others. You have seen the Lord in the miracle of healing and the miracle of comfort when sickness gave way to death. You have seen the Lord change lives, give hope, and heal marriages.

But sometimes, telling people we have seen the Lord seems to be in the same category as telling someone we have seen a UFO. There are so many who claim to be Christians, who claim to have seen the Lord, and, frankly, they embarrass the rest of us. Their lives either don't back up their testimony or are lives that no one else would want to live. So, even though seeing the Lord has made a sane and significant difference in our lives, it's just easier not to mention it.

Maybe that's one of the benefits of singing in the choir. We can tank up on air and courage and then "let 'er rip" (in *fortississimo* passages) because everyone else standing around us in choir is doing the same thing. Sing boldly, "I have seen the Lord." See the Lord in the task of the choir and the messages of the anthems. See the Lord in the healing work of the choir's music.

Saying "I have seen the Lord" is never less than a duet. The Lord you have seen at work in your life and in the lives of others around you is with you. Let your life say so and now and then it might even be comfortable and conversational to let your voice say so. That will surely be true on Sunday morning. Lilies, white robes, new shoes, big crowd—everything will be shouting, "I have seen the Lord!" Let the choir lead the way. Not just with the appropriate anthem, but also with lives that have been singing this same message all year long.

Prayer: "Dear God, the resurrection of Jesus makes it possible for us to experience springtime, no matter what circumstances have plunged us into winter. Thank you for the wonderful gift of hope. Amen."

Week 12 **Hymn:** *"I Am Thine, O Lord," stanza 2: "Let my soul look up with a steadfast hope, and my will be lost in thine," words by Fanny J. Crosby.*

We know that when we become Christians, the Holy Spirit comes to live in us. Yet, even when we bow our heads and bend our knees, our spirits look up. There is something about the presence of God the Son and God the Spirit that lifts up our heads and hearts. The Holy Spirit can cause a warmth and zeal in our souls that can sometimes best be described as a burning. I've know a few Christians in which that inner "burning" has caused their entire being, personality, and countenance to practically "glow." That's how the Holy Spirit startles us today. The startling presence of the Holy Spirit was more obvious still at Pentecost.

A fire in the sky will cause heads and hearts to look up. The fiery blast of jet engine afterburners at an air show or a comet passing through the night sky grabs our attention. But those examples don't hold a candle to the electrifying display we know as lightning. Those tongues of fire connecting the sky and the earth remind us how little we are and how big God is. Each lesson is an occurrence so bright and so powerful we are only allowed to observe it for an instant.

The Bible records some instances of human encounters with the presence of God. In those encounters, the actual countenance of God was shielded or veiled. Like a lightning strike, I suppose, the mortal human probably wouldn't be able to stand it. The person of Jesus and the person of the Holy Spirit are God in forms that we can embrace.

Conversation with Jesus, the Comforter, tongues of fire; the best we can do is echo the words of those who walked with Jesus on the road to Emmaus: "Were not our hearts burning within us while he was talking to us?" (Luke 24:32).

At Pentecost, everyone present, no matter what language they spoke, understood those preaching about Jesus. It's true of us, too, whether it is from the choir loft or our desk at work. God's love speaking through you will burn through any language barrier. Perhaps that love will then cause others to let their souls look up with a steadfast hope, and their wills to be lost in the Lord's.

Prayer: "Dear God, let your Holy Spirit glow through our lives and our songs. Amen."

Week 13

Scripture: *"The hour is coming, and is now when the true worshipers will worship the Father in spirit and truth, for the Father seeks such as these to worship him. God is spirit, and those who worship him must worship in spirit and truth" (John 4:23-24).*

On Sunday this choir will gather to worship and to lead in worship. Here are a couple of suggestions to take with you into the choir loft.
   1. Don't deny what this world has done to you this week, or what you have done to it.
   2. Don't deny the existence of the other world—your soul and its spiritual environment.

In other words, next Sunday, be sure that you worship truthfully and in the Spirit.

We enter the worship experience affected by all that we have experienced, whether in a lifetime or in the past week. To deny that is to be less than truthful as we bow in worship before the One who has instructed us to worship in truth. Yet, we are also less than truthful if we come before God's throne affected only by our earthly experiences. We are to worship in spirit as well as truth. When we acknowledge our spiritual existence a new world of hope and possibilities stretches out before us and around us. Worship allows the spiritual world to comment on and interpret the events of the physical world. God is in the midst of that conversation to let us know that God is sovereign in both worlds. God is truly worthy of worship.

That will be the setting in which your anthem and other musical involvements will be offered: real people trying to worship and weave together the realities of two worlds. Worship with them truthfully and in the Spirit. Between now and Sunday, watch to see how the message of Sunday's anthem speaks to the weaving of the two worlds in your life. Then sing out the message with confidence. Offer it as worship to God and testimony to the congregation. Sing in Spirit and in truth. This is the ministry to which you have been called and for which you have been gifted.

Before we know it, the entire living of our lives throughout the week joins tonight's singing as part of the rehearsal for the truthful and spiritual presentation of the anthem on Sunday. Maybe that explains the strange phrase in our scripture passage: "the hour is coming and is now here." Worship is not just a Sunday morning event.

Prayer: *"Dear God, help us to understand that preparation for worship is a form of worship in itself. Help us to not compartmentalize our lives into Sunday and the rest of the week, or spiritual and worldly. Help us to live and worship in Spirit and in truth. Amen."*

Summer

Hymn: *"Take My Life, and Let It Be,"* stanza 1: *"Take my moments and my days; let them flow in ceaseless praise,"* words by Frances R. Havergal.

You never know when one of a day's 1,440 minutes is going to turn out to be a *moment*—one of those defining or teaching or life-changing moments. It is a wise person who learns to live each minute in the knowledge that it has the potential of becoming such a moment.

Moments can occur anytime—during a choir rehearsal or during the choir's leadership in the worship event. The Holy Spirit brings new meaning to the text or music of an anthem, through both the singing of it and the hearing of it. While these moments cannot be manufactured, they can and should be anticipated. Happily, they are not confined to the rehearsal room or the choir loft.

When minutes turn into moments, we should take the time to thank God for them. They serve as little spiritual retreats. We do well to thank God every time God lets us know that we are not alone, or forgotten, or insignificant. When the Creator of the universe takes time to touch one of our moments, we should pause to say "thank you."

An interesting thing happens when we begin to expect and recognize minutes that have been transformed into moments: we begin to see more of them. Soon we are living lives of expectancy. A day is not something that happens inside our wristwatch—it is life, lived now and in the presence of the Holy Spirit. We start to understand the apostle Paul's admonition to pray without ceasing and the hymnwriter's belief that we can string together moments of praise like a ceaseless string of pearls.

For us, one of the arenas in which this "baptizing" of minutes becomes a stewardship responsibility is the choir. God has gifted us with voices and energy and minutes. God asks us to lead the congregation in worship; in the transformation of minutes into moments that can make the difference in a day or a lifetime.

Everyone has the same number of minutes in a day. Sadly, some people have very few moments. Through Jesus Christ, God stepped into time. Through the Holy Spirit, God transforms time. One moment in your life or in the life of a parishioner is worth the minutes you invest in rehearsal and in worship.

Prayer: "Dear God, take my moments and my days; let them flow in ceaseless praise. Help me to breathe deeply and be aware of your presence. In Jesus' name. Amen."

Week 15

Scripture: "*I thank my God every time I remember you, constantly praying with joy in every one of my prayers for all of you*" (*Phil. 1:3*).

What if the congregation had these kinds of thoughts throughout the week as they remembered the choir's contribution to the worship event? "Every time I remember you, I am encouraged." "Every time I remember you, my faith is strengthened." "Every time I remember you, I remember the wonderful worship experiences we have had together." Those would be wonderful echoes coming from the choir's Sunday morning presentation. It can happen.

Each choir member must remember that the choir is not a block of conjoined people who are freaks during the week, but quite at home in the choir loft on Sunday morning. A choir is made up of individuals who are recognizable even when robed and standing in the choir loft.

Before Paul's concept of "joy in every one of my prayers for all of you," we must deal with the individual matter of "every time I remember you." An unsettled dispute between you and an individual in the congregation will probably be all that is memorable to that person when you stand with the rest of the choir to sing. The choir's message and mission are too important for that stumbling block to go unresolved. We are as responsible for our relationships to individuals in the congregation as we are to individual notes on the score. It's not easy, but it is the mission God calls us to when we are given the gifts of salvation and song. How can we sing God's message to a person to whom we will not "give the time of day"? Rehearsing the soul as well as the music allows us to cultivate the listener and the anthem. Both need to be prepared if the choir's part of the worship event is to be memorable.

An important part of Paul's statement has to do with prayer. We are artists, even if our art has a specific function in the context of the church. Artists deal with talent and taste and dedicated rehearsal. Where does prayer fit into that?

Talent, like life, is fragile. This does not mean that we should pray in fear, as if God might take the talent away. It means that we should pray in thanksgiving for being the recipient of that talent. We should pray for the faith and strength to tend to the notes on the page and the persons in the pew.

In this rehearsal, envision Sunday's anthem helping to deposit yet another rich worship experience into the congregation's memory bank.

Prayer: "Dear God, help our lives and our songs to be sources of lasting encouragement, strength, and joy to those who hear us sing. In Jesus' name. Amen."

Week 16   *Hymn: "He Leadeth Me: O Blessed Thought,"*
stanza 2: "Sometimes mid scenes of deepest gloom,
―――――――― *sometimes where Eden's bowers bloom, by waters*
still, o'er troubled sea, still 'tis his hand that leadeth me," words by
Joseph H. Gilmore.

Some come leaping, some come limping, and some come in the stupor of routine. The gathering for worship becomes a rather bizarre collection of self-centered individuals. How can we coordinate and combine our focus? Modeling focus, purpose, and expectation, the choir can lead the diverse congregation to a unifying experience of worship.

The choir should not paste on uniform, manufactured smiles as part of their liturgical garb. Natural expressions growing out of individual struggles give an air of truthfulness. Yet, these individual pictures of truth can be unified in honest anticipation of real worship. The congregation will think they are looking in a mirror. They will see themselves rising above the week's successes and failures to focus on One who has kept the week's events in perfect perspective. This person is worthy of our worship. The choir can lead this congregation to worship when and if each member of the choir believes it and lives it.

The message the choir has to proclaim is one of the beauty of living life with Jesus as example and personal companion. Jesus has rowed across still waters and walked across turbulent waters. He is our example and companion. Sing it from lives that declare it to be true. People will come to worship leaping and limping and lethargic. Sing to them the good news of the ignored, unseen Companion who walked in beside them. You can do that when you realize that Jesus stands with you in the choir loft, having experienced your week with you. Live it and then sing it. The congregation needs you and your firsthand account.

Being led by the Lord is something to rehearse. Just as one must spend time "in the music" to properly rehearse for performance, so, too, must one spend time "in the Word," to study the life and ways of our example and companion, Jesus.

If everyone showed up for worship "leaping," our task would be simpler. But they don't. We sing the good news to all kinds of people who have had all kinds of experiences. On any given Sunday any one of us may stumble in, but we can be led out "by God's own hand." Sing to them the song.

Prayer: "Dear God, help us to admit to our individual needs. Help us to see the needs of others. Help us all to bow before your throne in worship and rise to be led by your hand. In Jesus' name. Amen."

Week 17

Why do things change so much and so often? Perhaps one of the reasons is that we are on a journey. The scenery is constantly changing when you are traveling from one place to another.

Sunday, you will be singing to people who are passing through and to those who are permanent residents. Summer is a time when many families move. Those who are about to move from your community or who have just moved into it are in the process of being uprooted and replanted. These people need to be reminded of what remains constant in their lives, what they can count on no matter where they live. They will be in your congregation for a sad last time or an exploratory first time.

What about the permanent residents? Their life, too, is a journey. They may be at the same old address, but they are travelers nonetheless. They are traveling through life's passages. They are there to say good-bye to those who are leaving and hello to those who are coming. What goes on in the privacy of that existence is the toughest journey of all.

You, like everyone else, must learn to deal with change. You sing in the choir that, once a week, has a chance (and the call) to show "the Lord sitting on a throne, high and lofty." People on a journey need to see that vision often. For you to know it and present it with integrity, you must see it and recognize it and call upon it in your own journey.

The death of King Uzziah was a big enough change that Isaiah used the event to identify a whole year. There may be an event or events in your life that are defining this year. You sing of the Lord directly or indirectly every week. Do you allow the melodies to filter each day's noise and keep the sounds in perspective? Are the words of the anthems part of the score that is stuck back into your folder, or do they go with you to cushion the blows of daily change and energize your routine? The business and ministry of your choir is an important part of the Sunday intersection of all these journeys. Trust the Lord's presence and guidance. Worship the Lord. Worship helps us energize our hearts for the journey. Sing to those at the rest stop under your steeple next Sunday. Sing to them of the consistent love of God. Keep a few notes and words back for yourself. You, too, are on a journey.

Prayer: "Dear God, sometimes life seems like constant change. We wonder, sometimes, what there is left that we can count on. Remind us through your word, your music, and your presence, that you are always with us. Help us to remind those we meet on the path. In Jesus' name. Amen."

Week 18   **Hymn:** *"All Praise to Thee, for Thou, O King Divine,"* stanza 4: *"Wherefore, by God's eternal purpose, thou art high exalted o'er all creatures now, and given the name to which all knees shall bow: Alleluia!"* words by F. Bland Tucker.

Our heritage, our identity, and a prediction of our future are wrapped up in just two or three words: our name. Interesting thought processes lead to the naming of children. More interesting still are the processes and events that lead to changing names.

It is customary for a married woman to change her last name to her husband's name, yet increasingly, she keeps her maiden name, or adds the husband's last name with a hyphen. Keeping Dad's name and adding a II, III, or IV on the end says a great deal about what that name means in family history. Through achievements of one sort or another, Sergeant, Lieutenant, Doctor, or Professor can become part of an individual's name. Nicknames are very telling.

In Daniel 12:1 we are introduced to the concept of our names being written in a heavenly book. The scripture also reports that the Lord knows my name. I wonder which of my names the Lord uses to identify me? What name does the Lord use to get my attention? There is a deep and hidden name that only the Lord knows. That's how I know when it is God speaking. God knows all my names, even that one, and still God loves me.

Some of the most interesting events in the biblical record are instances of person's names being changed. The Lord is constantly working on changing my name, refining it. My name is in the process of being made shorter and purer.

There will be a time when all knees and names bow before one name, the name of Jesus. It is a concept that cannot be fully communicated without singing. Someday, all I have been, am, and will be, will bow at the sound of that name. Lord, let me start rehearsing that today. The hymnic prayer, "tune my heart to sing Thy praise," is nothing more than an acknowledgment of the importance of rehearsing the soul and its many names for that great event. We shouldn't wait. "Wherefore, by God's eternal purpose, thou are high exalted o'er all creatures *now*."

When the choir sings, it models for those who come to worship the bowing of our many names before the One Name. The bowing before the name of Jesus ends and will endlessly end with alleluias.

Prayer: "Dear God, help us not to take the name of Jesus in vain, by word or deed. Help us even now to reverence the name and worship the person of Jesus. In his name we pray. Amen."

Scripture: "Create in me a clean heart, O God, and put a new and right spirit within me" (Ps. 51:10).

Rhetorical questions are a powerful way of making a point. For instance: "The Lord is my light and my salvation; whom shall I fear?" Answer: No one. "If God is for us, who can be against us?" Answer: No one. "God calls us to worship and the Holy Spirit helps us worship. Who then, can keep us from worshiping?" Answer: No one.

But each question, though meant to be rhetorical, may have another answer. Whom shall I fear? Who can be against me? Who can keep me from worshiping? Me. I can.

Our words and actions reflect our heart. That's why we are constantly rehearsing our souls. The psalmist knew this had to be the work of God. We can't make such fundamental changes on our own. God is the Creator, even of clean hearts.

We rehearse the music the director has chosen for the choir to sing. But there is another level of commitment related to our singing in the choir. It is a singer/Creator issue. "Create in me a clean heart, O God, and put a new and right spirit within me." The psalmist's prayer should be the choir member's prayer each time the choir gathers. There isn't much in the world that helps us prepare to sing in the church choir. In fact, the world probably thinks our church and choir involvement is a colossal waste of time and energy. We wade through that kind of environment every week to make our way back to this place, this task, this time of spiritual refreshing through music.

It is important to note, however, that if this place is the one and only oasis and sanctuary for us, we might not make it back. We must carry the oasis and sanctuary with us, in our hearts. The clean heart goes with us and is capable of constant renewal and strengthening. The right spirit that goes along with it can cut through the pressure that the world stacks up in the time and path between leaving here and returning here.

In the music you are rehearsing, find God's message to cleanse your heart and renew your spirit.

Prayer: "Dear God, my heart is in constant need of renewal and correction. Help me to focus on you and your presence, help me to focus on your word. Help me to take the message of tonight's music into tomorrow's challenges. In Jesus' name. Amen."

Week 20

Hymn: "I Come with Joy," stanza 1: "I come with joy to meet my Lord, forgiven, loved and free, in awe and wonder to recall his life laid down for me," words by Brian Wren.

This morning, two minutes before the clock radio was to sound, the beautiful and persistent song of a bird awakened me. This day and my awakening to it were the work of God.

So, too, with that eternal day and our awakening to it; it is not our doing, but God's. The observance of Holy Communion (Eucharist or the Lord's Supper) is the beautiful and persistent song that wakes us up to that fact—it is God's doing.

When even something this special is experienced over and over again, it can easily be forgotten that each experience and what it represents are gifts. Gifts should not be accepted lightly or without notice.

These thoughts are not comments on frequency of observance; they are comments on thoughtless observance. To remember the shed blood and broken body of Jesus is to be reminded that we are "forgiven, loved and free."

Awe and wonder can be woven into the choir's music and presentation of that music. But, it needs to be rehearsed. During rehearsal, the music starts to come together with the words. The words start to burrow into our hearts and the entire experience becomes an awe-inspiring source of wonder. If that hasn't happened yet, the piece is not ready, and you are not ready.

Dietrich Bonhoeffer wrote, "It is by the grace of God that a congregation is permitted to gather visibly in this world to share God's Word and sacrament" (*Life Together,* New York: Harper & Row, 1954, p.18). Bonhoeffer wrote those words in a Nazi prison camp just days before he was executed. When we gather together, we are strengthened and encouraged. When we gather around the Table, the presence of Christ is even more apparent and we remember what this family is all about. It has past, present, and future significance. Don't just sing past it like so many measures of duty completed. Taste each note and word as if it were bread and wine.

If you can experience this awe and wonder in rehearsal, you will have much more to contribute on Sunday.

Oh, that our lives might be awakened more often by birds than by alarm clocks. Oh, that our notes and words would more often be bread and wine.

Prayer: "Dear God, fill my life with a sense of awe and wonder at your great love for me. In Jesus' name. Amen."

Week 21 **Hymn:** *"Praise to the Lord, the Almighty," stanza 1: "Praise to the Lord, the Almighty, the King of creation! O my soul, praise him, for he is thy health and salvation! All ye who hear, now to his temple draw near; join me in glad adoration!" words by Joachim Neander.*

Frightening isn't it—our weakness against the strength of the world? But on Sunday we will gather to worship the almighty: the All Mighty.

I keep a picture handy. It is a picture of the Eagle Nebula taken through the *Hubble Space Telescope.* The picture itself is not big, but the subject of the picture is vast beyond comprehension. These light-year-tall stalagmites of gas and baby stars seem to be straining and stretching and bursting to shout the Creator's praise. I'd get a poster-sized picture of it for my office, but I'd never get any work done. The Almighty, the King of creation is my soul's health and salvation.

Who is in your midst when "God" is in your midst on Sunday mornings? Is the God who created the Eagle Nebula and the eagle's egg the same God who knows your heart and your "to do list"? Is the God who walked through the black patches of our night sky to create tens of thousands of galaxies we cannot see without the *Hubble* the same God who walks through the doors of your sanctuary on Sundays? Yes!

Who God is and how big God is does not change with our acknowledgment or ignorance of God. What changes is the size of our life and our environment and our hope. Take God for granted and your world shrinks. Get a glimpse of who God is and your universe expands. Realize God is right beside you and you walk on top of the world. Ignore God's presence and the weight of the world crushes you. Why do we so often choose to feel alone and small when God's presence is available to stretch our vision and expand our awareness? God has promised to be in the midst of the two or three who will gather for worship on Sunday. Now how important is this rehearsal?

Our songs must serve to expand our hearts and minds and imaginations. Sing with the Eagle Nebula and the manger in your heart. Sing from your tiny piece of dirt at the foot of the cross and the night sky. Sing praise to the Lord, the Almighty, the King of creation, who is also your health and salvation!

Prayer: "Dear Lord, now and then, give me a glimpse of your vastness. Always keep me aware of your presence. In Jesus' name. Amen."

Week 22   ***Scripture:*** *"Singers and dancers alike say, 'All my springs are in you' " (Ps. 87:7).*

The fact that you like to sing may get you into choir, but it won't keep you there. There must be more to motivate you to be faithful to the weekly rehearsals, the "bonus" rehearsals, and weekly worship leadership. The joy of singing won't keep you in the music when you think the anthem ought to be given to the youth choir or the shredder. If enthusiasm and commitment are to be sustained, they must ultimately bubble up from one spring. That spring is the Lord and our love for the Lord.

Flat tires, headaches, soccer practice, just plain fatigue, and overload say something has to give. Why not choir? They won't miss your one mediocre voice. At times like that we need to revisit the fountain.

Our scripture reference groups the choir with the dance troupe. I like that. Singers and dancers are kindred spirits. The psalmist says that the dancers are in the same boat as the singers. They can't keep going without frequent visits to the spring.

Refreshment for singing, dancing, living, hanging in there. "All my springs," says the psalmist, "are in you." The writer is talking to our Lord. The truth is eternal. We can do our weekly dance routine of rehearsals and performance in the midst of smothering responsibilities because we've been to the spring.

Have you begun to see choir rehearsal as a spring yet? It can be. Be aware of that and be refreshed by it. When that happens you will waltz into choir rehearsal, expecting to get your face wet and your soul-thirst quenched. That kind of expectation is usually rewarded.

Even when we're not thirsty, there's something about the sound of a spring. It sings to us that we can get a drink anytime we want to. Drinking from the spring and listening to the spring are accompanied by the sheer pleasure of watching light dance on the water.

When they leave the worship center next Sunday let the "Singers and dancers alike say, 'All my springs are in you.' "

Prayer: "Dear God, continue to bubble up in my life. I need your living water and refreshing presence. Lord, let some of it splash out on those around me, until they find the spring for themselves. In Jesus' name. Amen."

Week 23   *Hymn:* "Savior, Like a Shepherd Lead Us," stanza 1: "Savior, like a shepherd lead us, much we need thy tender care," words by Dorothy A. Thrupp.

Our daily lives do not bring us into contact with shepherds. Yet, we love the image of a shepherd. Perhaps that's because we know our need of guidance and protection. Even in worship we need a shepherd. We need a shepherd to guide us to God and to protect us from distractions. The Lord is our Shepherd first and foremost. Our pastor is also a shepherd. Our choir director is a shepherd. We, too, are shepherds. The choir has its opportunities in the course of a worship experience to do some shepherding. The choir can show the congregation the path to working together for a common goal. The choir can shepherd the congregation toward participation in hymn singing. The messages of the anthems speak of and for the Shepherd.

All of us need to be aware of the times and situations in which we need shepherding and in which we are called to be shepherds. It's a learning process that is part of being one of Jesus' disciples. Everyone walks through the "valley of the shadow of death." Sometimes that is literal; sometimes the death is the death of a dream or a relationship. If we are the ones knocked down we need a shepherd to lift us up. If we are the ones still standing, we need to do the lifting.

Dorothy Thrupp, in her hymn, admitted that we need the Savior's tender care. It is good for us to sing those words. It is better still for us to adopt the words as our very own prayer. Through Bible study, devotional reading, and prayer, we can become aware of the presence of the Spirit of Jesus at our side constantly. Do you go through your daily routine with a sense that Jesus is there with you? I believe that awareness should be the norm for Christians, not the exception.

A choir of obedient Christ-followers who are aware of Jesus' presence in their lives and in the choir loft will go a long way in effective shepherding. Their caring spirits will go out to the congregation along with the anthem.

We need the Shepherd's leadership. We need his tender care. The Lord is our Shepherd. Listen for the Shepherd's voice. Sing the Shepherd's song.

Prayer: "Dear God, thank you for your presence in our daily lives. Forgive us for taking you for granted and for ignoring you. Help us to live strengthened and radiant lives. In Jesus' name. Amen."

Scripture: "Your people shall be my people, and your God my God" (Ruth 1:16b).

Yes, it's true, our scripture passage is taken from Ruth's statement of devotion to her mother-in-law, Naomi. But it is holy scripture and can easily be applied to our work as choir members. "Your people shall be my people" should be our prayer to God, and "your God my God" should be our sacred trust with the congregation.

The choir does not sing *to* the congregation. The choir sings *with* them and at times *for* them. Therefore, one of our driving commitments must be to see each person and each life in the pews as God sees them. It means we will share the Good News with them when we are too tired. It also means that we will make every effort to know them, care for them, and be there for them outside the choir loft. God never leaves or ceases to care for God's people. "God's people shall be my people." It is very difficult to sing of God's love for these people from the choir loft if you would rather not speak to them. You and the message in your charge are a package. This is why the soul must be as well and freshly rehearsed as the voice; why the message must be as ingrained in us as the music.

God deserves to hear our prayer: "Your people shall be my people." It is also true that the congregation deserves to hear (in word and in deed) our commitment: "Your God [is] my God." We should never be involved in trying to convince the congregation of something we don't believe. We should never point them toward a God we do not know, do not trust, do not believe in. The congregation must know that we seek God and seek to be obedient with the same intensity as our music implies and encourages.

How then can we give ourselves to ever deepening and refined love for the people and obedience to God? It begins with seeing choir rehearsal as a time of spiritual renewal and Sunday's anthem as a time of worship and worship leadership instead of seeing them as two "gigs."

Ruth also said to Naomi, "Where you die, I will die—there will I be buried" (1:17*a*). Jesus died for the people in the congregation, even the difficult ones. Will you "die to self" and "bury" yourself in the Christlike work of loving the congregation, and helping them worship?

Prayer: "Dear God, I want to love you more deeply. I acknowledge that that will mean going out of my way to love your people. I give myself to you and to the work for which you have gifted me and called me. In Jesus' name. Amen."

Hymn: "On Eagle's Wings," refrain: "And God will raise you up on eagle's wings, . . . and hold you in the palm of God's [His] hand," words by Michael Joncas.

I awoke early to do my morning walk. On this particular day, it was along the shore of a beautiful lake. During the walk, I watched birds in flight. They flew in formation: four ducks and the Spirit. Their demonstration rivaled those of the Thunderbirds and the Blue Angels. Without radio communication or flight plan, they soared and swooped and made beautiful low-level, high-speed passes. They were flying for the pure joy of flight. In dawn's early glimmer, above the lake's mist, they experienced the joy of flight, the blessing of freedom in and with the Spirit.

You've experienced it, too, in the soaring of the music—when the composer's dream, the choir's voices, and the Holy Spirit have flown in beautiful formation from the choir loft, out over the congregation, and finally, landed softly in the hearts of everyone present. The air and atmosphere practically shone with the Spirit's presence and there was a holy hush after the cutoff in which even a whispered "amen" would have seemed sacrilege.

We can't manufacture such moments. But we can ask why they don't occur more often. That's what worship ought to be like, if not every time, then at least more often than not. Why are such moments the exception rather than the rule?

The answer to our question may lie in the words of our hymn, which is based on Exodus 19:4. "And *God* will raise you up on eagle's wings." Those times of soaring don't come because we rehearsed that particular piece harder than others. The experience is more than the result of a tried-and-true formula of chord progressions, dynamics, and modulations. If either of those scenarios was the source of our soaring, we could manufacture "Xeroxed" experiences every time we sing. Something else happens in those occasional special moments. God is the source of the soaring. Our responsibility is to continue to worship. Now and then, God touches the moment and we soar with the music and the spirit. Perhaps God is letting us know how it feels and sounds to God. There is joy enough for us in participating in the act of worship out of love and reverence for God.

God will fly in formation with you. God will hold you up in the palm of God's hand. Let your singing and your spirit soar. Give the congregation soaring lessons.

Prayer: "Dear God, help me to rely on you more and more. Help me to expect to be lifted up and sustained by your hand. Through our singing, help the congregation to find their wings. In Jesus' name. Amen."

Fall

Scripture: "I have fought the good fight, I have finished the race, I have kept the faith" (2 Tim. 4:7).

The term "finishing line" has always seemed a misnomer to me. If you *don't* make it to the finishing line you are finished. If you *do* make it to the finishing line, first or last, you find it to be an opening to new opportunities.

Perhaps collapsing into your chair in choir rehearsal tonight was like making it across a finishing line with your last ounce of energy. Now the choir director wants you to attack the music with enthusiasm and energy. Where has he or she been all day?

So many times today you've had the chance to throw in the towel, and out of sheer determination, responsibility, or habit, you did what it took to get the job done. Why? Because deep down inside you know it is ultimately worth it. You'd just like a little recognition or a little help along the way.

At least choir rehearsal is a chance to sit down and be still for awhile. You're not in charge so you can relax a bit. But there's something about this place, these people, and the music. There's something right and refreshing about choir and choir rehearsal. It was a hassle to get here and you almost didn't come, but now that you're here, there's just something right about it all.

It may be that choir rehearsal is a "right" place to be once a week because it is a reminder that you are not alone. There are other people pushing their way through the week. Their busy schedules also include this place and time. It is a reminder that you have some eternal work to do in the midst of your daily responsibilities. It is a time to look up and out over the horizon, instead of just looking out to make sure you don't get run over. It is a time to use your voice for something other than answering questions or giving instructions. It is a time to harmonize instead of shouting to be heard. It is touching home base before running back out into the race. At the end of rehearsal there is the feeling that you have made progress. That feeling doesn't come as often as we would like during the week. Most of all, choir rehearsal is a time to remember that God is with you. That helps you keep the pace and keep the faith.

Prayer: "Dear God, I'm tired. Sometimes, even often, I wonder if what I'm doing is worth it. Please renew my strength and my faith. Help me to remember that you are with me. Help me to see my part of the big picture through your eyes. In Jesus' name, Amen."

Scripture: *"For where two or three are gathered in my name, I am there among them" (Matt. 18:20).*

It's an environment in which we learn to handle joys and jealousies, sorrows and celebrations, hugs and hassles. It is, of course, family.

Our society has come to use the word *family* in a broader sense. In addition to those who have our blood and/or street address, we now think of family as those who share common interests, commitment, and geography, no matter their lineage or heritage. I like that. Choirs are a family in the broader sense, and that's good. Have you ever noticed how families seem larger on holidays? Thanksgiving, Christmas, sometimes even Easter brings family members out of the woodwork. Some of them we haven't seen since the last big holiday. In the family setting at home, that's usually a reason for great rejoicing. In the family setting called choir, it can be a point of frustration. Where in the world have all those people been during the rest of the year?

"Where two or three are gathered in my name, I am there among them." That covers duets and trios, so it surely covers our choir. Being aware of Jesus' presence has an effect on families that are centered on him. Christ's presence forces us to remember his teachings and life example. When the prodigals return with the cool weather, Jesus' presence forces us to remember the parable.

Seeing ourselves and one another through Jesus' eyes will cause us to be closer and more loving. That helps the music we produce. It is as if the Holy Spirit hums along, adding a spiritual pedal point to our harmony. The Holy Spirit can take our one song and customize the hearing of it for the application needed in each heart in the church family. Look around at those in choir rehearsal tonight. They are family. Jesus died for each of them and promised to sit in with the group. Enjoy the fellowship. Be in awe of God's grace. Be aware of Jesus' presence, and thank God for the family.

Prayer: "Dear God, thank you for your presence with us. Thank you for our families, all of them. Forgive us for our self-centeredness. Help others to see and hear Jesus in us. We pray this in the presence and in the name of Jesus. Amen."

Week 28 **Hymn:** *"Come, Thou Fount of Every Blessing,"* stanza 2: *"Here I raise mine Ebenezer; hither by thy help I'm come," words by Robert Robinson.*

Life is filled with questions. "Why?" "What's next?" "Where do I fit in the universe?" and "What's an Ebenezer?" The last one isn't one of your life questions? The answer may be one of the biggest answers in your life.

The prophet Samuel had called all of Israel together to offer sacrifices to God and to repent. The Philistines heard about this prayer meeting and thought it would be a great time to attack Israel. When the people of Israel heard about the planned attack they asked Samuel to add protection from the Philistines to the prayer list. God answered the prayer: "The LORD thundered with a mighty voice that day against the Philistines and threw them into confusion" (1 Sam. 7:10). To commemorate the Lord's intervention and the ensuing victory, "Samuel took a stone and set it up between Mizpah and Jeshanah, and named it Ebenezer; for he said, 'Thus far the LORD has helped us.' " (1 Sam. 7:12).

Now we see that our question, "What's an Ebenezer?" is answered by the hymn itself: "hither by they help I'm come." That is the answer that can loom so big in our life experience and story. If you are still on your feet after coming through some difficult times, you can declare, "hither by thy help I'm come." If seemingly insurmountable circumstances have faded away and become history, say to God, "hither by thy help I'm come."

Every time the body of Christ gathers to worship, it is an Ebenezer experience. The entire congregation can shout in unison, "hither by thy help I'm come." Some will have experienced great joy and successes. Others will have endured times of deep sorrow and trial. Still others will have glimpsed little moments of the touch of God's hand in what would have otherwise been dulling routine. All can shout and sing, "hither by thy help I'm come."

The choir needs to lead the song. The choir, in its ministerial role, can wake the bruised, numb, and frightened, as well as those who may be entertaining the idea that their joy and success were their own doing. Hither, by God's help, they've come. Sing it. Know it yourself and remind the congregation.

Prayer: "Dear God, we praise you for your strength, guidance, and protection. Forgive us when we take your presence in our lives for granted. Help us to know and to teach through our singing that we get as far as we get because of your help. Tonight, we gratefully raise another Ebenezer. In Jesus' name. Amen."

Week 29 **Hymn:** *"Make Me a Captive, Lord," stanza 1: "Make me a captive, Lord, and then I shall be free," words by George Matheson.*

Which one of you showed up for choir rehearsal tonight? The master or the servant?

It seems as if the pressures of pace and responsibility force us to take over as much of our lives as possible. It's almost an act of survival to grasp for as much control as possible. Being Christ-followers and having some control over our schedules, we have decided to be at choir rehearsal tonight. But who showed up? The master of their life or the servant of the Lord? The answer matters because it will affect how you approach the music to be rehearsed and the worship to be led.

When in control, we learn for the sake of our agenda and goals. As servants, we learn for the sake of the master's agenda and goals. When we are in control we will approach the music we rehearse as an assignment we have accepted. If there is anything in it that can help us on toward accomplishing our agenda, we will internalize it. If, however, it's just the next song in the folder with no apparent good in it for us, we simply sing it. The servant, on the other hand, will approach the music to be rehearsed as the next lesson to be learned or assignment to be completed. Such learning will help us on toward Christlikeness and will build up the church.

Our worshiping and worship leadership will be affected by how we perceive our bondage. Bound to our own agenda and watching out for ourselves, we will approach worship looking for what we can get out of it. "Is it worth my time as a worshiper?" "Will our singing be a good performance, redeeming something from the otherwise boring hour?"

If our worshiping is that of a servant bowing before his or her master, we will lead the congregation humbly, expecting to worship *with* them rather than doing something *for* them or *to* them. Our worship is something that is offered to God and any "results" are God's doing. We don't have to manufacture anything or evaluate the experience by some success-oriented measuring stick. "Make me a captive, Lord, and then I shall be free."

Prayer: "Dear God, as we rehearse tonight, help us to listen to the message of the anthems as servants listening to their master. Help us to exchange our agendas for yours. Help us to pray, 'Your will, not mine.' Help us to live in the fullness of your grace. In Jesus' name. Amen."

Week 30 **Hymn:** *"Morning Has Broken," stanza 1: "Morning has broken like the first morning; ...Praise for them, springing fresh from the Word!" words by Eleanor Farjeon.*

The opening of a new anthem is like a dawning. Sometimes the sun rises on a good day, full of happy surprises; sometimes it rises on a day of unimagined setbacks. Sometimes, upon being introduced to a new anthem, we have to pray under our breath, "Lord, help me through this. Help me to see why you've brought this song and me together." Similarly, we might do well to approach each new day with the prayer, "Lord, help me to see what you have for me to learn and experience today. That approach to new music and new days can turn some questionable ones into favorites.

Let's continue this parallel line of thought. Most people don't sing in the choir. They're either in the congregation or at home. It's also true that most people never see the dawn. They're either in the house in bed or getting ready or they are already at work. The choir can become people of the "morning" who report to the larger crowd the beauty and hope of the dawn. The music and message dawns on the choir first and they stand in the choir loft on Sundays to report the glory of it. Morning people breathe the freshest air and see the clearest sky. The song of the birds is not yet drowned out in the mornings. The dew has not yet been stomped or scorched. Morning people have time with God before the crowds push in.

First, become a morning person for yourself. This doesn't necessarily mean that you have to set your alarm clock to go off an hour earlier. It does mean that you let God's light dawn on you, whenever and often. You learn to watch for the first rays. You listen to the birds as if they were the first bird of the morning. You can rehearse this awareness of the dawn in choir rehearsal. Each new song, whether it brings whistling or struggling, is a dawn, a morning experience. Praise God for the singing. Praise God for the morning.

Life-changing dawns and liberating mornings are to be found in the life and ministry of Jesus. Become people of the morning.

Prayer: "Dear God, thank you for the beauty of the morning. Thank you for all light that breaks into our darkness. Help us to live in and reflect your light. In Jesus' name. Amen."

The words of this great hymn remind me of the scripture that tells us how we are to love God: with all our heart, soul, mind, and strength. I'm even reminded of how we are to worship: in spirit and in truth. Combine all this and we have quite a list: heart, hands, voices, soul, mind, strength, spirit, and truth. If this list describes how we are to approach our thankfulness, love, and worship, it also does a good job of encompassing the work of the choir.

But who ever has that entire list together? Sometimes "voices" is the only item on the list that we can drag into choir rehearsal or Sunday's worship experience.

The choir loft is often a hospital for those strugglers who happen to be able to sing. Sometimes some of its members will indeed be singing from positions of spiritual strength. But sometimes the choir can only sing *about* spiritual maturity and strength. In those times, the choir may be voicing the prayers of the congregation more honestly than at any other time.

Even when hearts are broken, hands are tired, voices are hoarse from the day's shouting, minds are "wiped out," strength is used up, spirits are weak, and truth has been stretched to the point of warping, even in those times we are to worship God and lead others to worship God. We bring to God the best we have even when it is bruised and battered. In choir rehearsal, we work to salvage the best of what we dragged in to the rehearsal room.

God the Creator, the Redeemer, and the Comforter is good at mending brokenness, restoring strength, and bringing light to darkness. The soul needs to be rehearsed from time to time because the daily performances are so demanding. God knows the songs we most need to rehearse. All that is within us should praise the Lord, not just the part that still has a bit of shine to it.

"Show me your hand," Jesus said. Only then did he restore it from its withered state to wholeness. Maybe we need to "show our hand" more honestly to God as we rehearse, allowing the message of our anthems to enter our soul.

Our prayer comes from stanza 2 of our hymn for this week.

Prayer: "O may this bounteous God through all our life be near us, with ever joyful hearts and blessed peace to cheer us; and keep us still in grace, and guide us when perplexed; and free us from all ills, in this world and the next. Amen."

Week 32

Hymn: "Guide Me, O Thou Great Jehovah," stanza 1: "Guide me, O thou great Jehovah, pilgrim through this barren land. I am weak, but thou art mighty; hold me with thy powerful hand," words by William Williams.

Follow the Leader is still a popular children's game. It is also a good way for us to approach our call to be salt, light, and worship leaders. God led us here. "No," you may say, "Pure habit led me here. My car knows the day and the way." I still maintain that God led us here by way of our talent, our commitment, our love for music, and our need to be together now and then.

When we were kids and got to be the leader, we did as many silly and daring things as we could dream up to make it difficult for the kids behind us to follow. Not so with Jehovah. Jehovah may lead us to daring things, but not silly things. And no matter where Jehovah leads, Jehovah is there to give us strength.

Jehovah's guidance has us face the rigors of raising a family. Jehovah's guidance has us stand up to heartbreak and disappointment. Jehovah's guidance leads us into times of great challenge and even difficulty. Yet, we seem to make it through. Often those around us can't figure out how we made it. Often we don't know. We are weak, but God is mighty. God holds us with God's mighty hand.

It makes sense to follow a leader like that. Even though the "going" may be tough, our leader goes with us and gives us what we need for the journey.

Jehovah led you here. Jehovah will nudge you when you are singing something that you need to "pack away" for the journey. You came to rehearsal to get the music ready. Jehovah came to get you ready. Jehovah knows what's in the path just ahead.

God will lead you through the world that awaits you just outside the doors. God will lead you to and through the worship service on Sunday. God doesn't really send us, God goes with us and guides us. We are not alone. We are not on an unknown path. Our leader is the Light, even when we seem to be walking in the middle of the night. Following this leader will not be a test of our agility or bravery, but simply an exercise in faith and obedience. And the leader is our helper.

Sometimes, along the path, we get hungry for silence, for rest, for companionship, for meaning. "Bread of Heaven, feed me till I want no more."

Prayer: "Dear God, give me the faith and the strength to follow the Leader, even when the way is hard and the direction is confusing. Help me to follow the Leader, even when the way seems easy. Thank you for the hope of 'landing safe on Canaan's side.' In Jesus' name, Amen."

Week 33

Hymn: "I'll Praise My Maker While I've Breath," stanza 1: "I'll praise my Maker while I've breath; and when my voice is lost in death, praise shall employ my nobler powers. My days of praise shall ne'er be past, while life and thought, and being last, or immortality endures," words by Isaac Watts.

The veil between life and death, between this life and the next, between the physical world and the spiritual world, is thin indeed. Yet, we cannot reach through it. We can, however, connect with the "other side." We connect through prayer. Through prayer we connect with God who, while inhabiting our souls, stands just on the other side of the veil.

Our singing is a prayer. Music exists in this world and the next. Does knowledge of this connection inform our singing on this side? When we sing praise to God, we are engaging in a heavenly activity. If tonight we are rehearsing for Sunday, then Sunday we are rehearsing for heaven. It makes heaven, though still mysterious, a little more familiar. Singing God's praise; a foretaste, a preview, a prelude, and a connection. We know it comes from the soul, yet is a physical action. In heaven, the soul will be intact and the physical will be transformed into something much better. Our singing will automatically improve with its nobler power, but the soul and the song will be the same. Our singing is a connection.

Autumn seems to be a time of dying. Crops are chopped down and buried in bins and silos. Leaves fall off trees. The fall and the following winter, as deathlike as they may seem, are the seasons of our most beloved holidays. Family, feasting, joy: sounds a bit like heaven doesn't it? The veil is so thin that light seems to seep through now and then. Our singing is like a rainbow with one end on this side and the other end on the other side.

Now rehearse the music in your folder. We are leaning on the veil when we are singing and there seems to be a faint, but warm, echo to it now.

This is not the only world. It is, in fact, the lesser of the two. This is not the only life. It is the shorter of the two. The distance between is measured in heartbeats. Our rehearsal is preparation for reaching across to the other side.

Prayer: "Dear God, thank you for the hope of heaven. Thank you for music that rises above our circumstance and calls us upward. We praise you and thank you in Jesus' name. Amen."

Week 34

Scripture: "He must increase, but I must decrease" (John 3:30).

We are constantly pushed to increase. Increase productivity at work, increase our income, increase the size of our house, increase our retirement savings, increase our leisure time, increase the number of channels we can get on our TV. It's the American way. But it is not the way of the Christ-follower.

Increasing the volume of our voice can be motivated by the need to shout or to experience the satisfaction of having our talent recognized—two needs that are often brought on by how we are treated by the world. But our singing in choir should not be a world-motivated enterprise.

If I am to grow as a Christ-follower, I must be always moving toward "Christlikeness." His influence and lifestyle will become more prominent in our lives and we will increasingly "die to self." He will increase, we will decrease. It will affect our singing.

We spend so much time and energy (rightly so) on getting the music right, we fall prey to the possibility of losing sight of the "why" of it all. Keeping the "why" in sight is not license for sloppy performances. It is another reason for singing the best we possibly can. The "why" is this, "He must increase." Jesus is worthy of right notes and right hearts.

Choir is a corporate undertaking with only one person in charge. Choir is a constant exercise in decreasing the "I." As Jesus' place in our lives increases, and our desires decrease in importance, the soul is enriched. The soul is where our music takes on its spiritual significance. The decreasing "I" is good for our music.

Isn't it interesting that what is good for our souls is also good for our singing? It's because in the choir setting, all that is woven together. We know the importance of crescendos and decrescendos. We know the importance of strong voices and weaker voices blending together. Simply put, those musical facts are in the context of God's truth about Jesus and us, "He must increase, but I must decrease."

Prayer: "Dear God, thank you for how you have created and blessed personhood. Help me to respond humbly to that gift. Help others to see and hear Jesus in me. It is in his name I pray, Amen."

Week 35

Scripture: *"He put before them another parable: 'The kingdom of heaven is like a mustard seed that someone took and sowed in his field; it is the smallest of all the seeds, but when it has grown it is the greatest of shrubs and becomes a tree, so that the birds of the air come and make nests in its branches' " (Matt. 13:31-32).*

I love to visit places like the Carlsbad Caverns and the Grand Canyon. While the "oohs" and "aahs" are still echoing in the chambers of the giant stalactites and stalagmites, I like to look in the little, out-of-the-way nooks and crannies at the very small and unnoticed formations. God made them, too. Why? While others are dizzily moving back away from the edge of the Grand Canyon, I like to focus way across the wide expanse at a lone tree or boulder. They get lost is the larger awesome sight, but God made them, too. Why?

Similar thought processes could be applied to a single note in an oratorio, even in next Sunday's anthem. One little note. How big a deal is it? In the music of the masters, every note counts. The inevitability of each note is often mentioned in discussions of Mozart's music. That simply means that every note in his music is exactly the right note in the right place. No other note, no other placement would have been as strong, as inspired.

There must be countless millions of little examples of God's wondrous design that go unnoticed. It is easy to think, sometimes, that maybe I am one of them. In the overall, big picture of life on this planet (in this universe?), you have to look very carefully to see me. I'm as small as a mustard seed in a farmer's field.

The little mustard seed in Jesus' parable grows into a tree. That tree ends up being exactly the right size and in exactly the right location for a bird to use it as a nesting site. Pretty noble contribution for a little seed.

How about the little note in next Sunday's anthem?

There is a word or at least a syllable under that little note. It may well be the word or part of the word that will give rest to a weary soul. Do your best to be and sing the part God has given you.

Prayer: "Dear God, please forgive me for the times I think too highly or too lowly of myself. Help me to see myself as your creation, existing for and at your pleasure. I am yours. Use me according to your plan and purpose. In Jesus' name. Amen."

Week 36

Can people tell who your teacher is? Often a choir's approach to choral technique can easily be traced back to a particular origin. Those origins include Robert Shaw, Fred Warring, St. Olaf College, Westminster Choir College, and so on. A trained ear can often tell who a choir director's teacher is.

When the Pharisees approached Jesus' disciples, they didn't have to ask who their teacher was. They could tell by the way they acted. When you focus on the teachings and habits of a particular person, you begin to assume into your own "style" their habits, responses, and attitudes. You will eventually learn how your choir director thinks and what he or she wants in certain musical situations. You anticipate how your choir director will react based on past experiences (by the way, that's what pencils are for).

In our context, the questions "Who is your teacher?" and "Who is your choir's teacher?" are focused on whether your answer is "A musician" or "The Master." You can tell if a church choir's teacher is one of the choral "gurus." You can also tell if a church choir's teacher is the Master. If your choir's teacher is a musician only, the music will be obviously chosen and performed for music's sake. If your choir also learns from the Master, your beautiful and technically correct music will graciously point to God. Who is your teacher? It matters.

Like the disciples, you may be questioned about the actions and directions of your teacher. When your teacher leads you to perform an anthem that is well done, but would not be heard in a performing arts center, the Pharisees may corner you. "Why does your teacher eat with sinners?"

We want the affirmation of our peers. But in a church choir setting, we have goals above purely musical principles.

A church choir is made up of human beings, sinners, who are trying in worship and in life to act more like their teacher. Getting the notes right is very important, but may be the easiest of all that we are rehearsing.

Prayer: "Dear God, it is our prayer that in our singing and in our living, others will see Jesus in us. We pray that his words and his voice will be heard each time we perform and lead in worship. We want it to be obvious that Jesus is our teacher. It is in his name we pray, Amen."

Week 37

Scripture: "Then the LORD God formed man from the dust of the ground, and breathed into his nostrils the breath of life; and the man became a living being" (Gen. 2:7).

Have you ever experienced the performance of an anthem that turned out to be far better than it deserved to be? It didn't sound that good at the last rehearsal, but it seemed to come to life in worship. No doubt you have had that experience. You've probably also been in rehearsals in which you've just finished singing an anthem and there is silence. No one dares to talk, because everyone knows there was something very special about what was just sung. Somehow at that moment, the anthem took on a life of its own. In both instances, we know that what happened was more than right notes, proper enunciation, and good blend.

We pray that God will always inspire the hearing of our anthems in worship. Now and then we are certain that God has inspired the singing. God does breathe life into otherwise dead things. Those moments remind us that we are "about our Father's business." We are reminded that the One we worship actually helps us worship.

If music can "come alive," how about the existence of a person who is already breathing? Sometimes we can feel like overworked robots. We even have phrases in our language such as "dead on my feet" and "dead-end job." Can God still breathe life into my existence? A robot programmed to say "Life is wonderful" isn't very convincing.

People experiencing stress or distress are often advised to breathe deeply. Choir members who rush in to rehearsal at the last second or later, jumping off the day's runaway treadmill, need the breathing exercises that choir affords, both physically and spiritually. Interestingly, the music often breathes life into us before we can breathe life into it. The process of the music inspiring us and then us inspiring the music is a form of inhaling and exhaling in itself. God can breathe life into that kind of a rehearsal. The weary choir member can be resuscitated in that kind of environment.

Prayer: "Dear God, breathe life into our dead lives and deadening routines. Bring our music to life through the fresh breeze of your spirit. Lord, through us make Sunday's time of worship a resuscitating experience for those who come into the sanctuary out of breath. In Jesus' name. Amen."

Week 38 **Scripture:** *"Therefore, my beloved, be steadfast, immovable, always excelling in the work of the Lord, because you know that in the Lord your labor is not in vain" (1 Cor. 15:58).*

If you have never wondered whether or not your being in choir matters; whether or not you are accomplishing anything, then you haven't been a choir member very long. It takes effort to be a good choir member. It also takes a little biting of your lip now and then when the choir director hands you a piece of music that you would never select if it were up to you. Church is pretty much the same year in and year out. Choir members join, choir members drop out. What's it all about anyway? You like to sing, but it's not like you don't have anything else to do. Does my involvement matter or have I just become part of the church's wallpaper?

In our scripture for today we are assured that our work for the Lord is not in vain. The problem is, we don't see a tally sheet at the end of a worship service or a month or a year. It would be nice to know that we encouraged 6.4 percent more congregates this year than we did last year. It would be nice if there was an "Inspired-o-Meter" in the back of the sanctuary so we could get a reading on our performance after the anthem.

It is important for us to remember that much if not all of God's work of inspiration, healing, and encouragement happens in the soul, the unseen inner reaches of the person's being. Our work for the Lord is, after all, just that—for the Lord. What God does with it in the lives of others is up to God. We should offer our best to God whether God uses it in the lives of others or absorbs it all and keeps it.

Our work in the Lord is an act of love, commitment, and obedience. We are aware that people benefit from it, but we are not to measure its success in terms of business product and profit. "Therefore, my beloved [choir member], be steadfast, immovable, always excelling in the work of the Lord, because you know that in the Lord your labor is not in vain."

Prayer: "Dear God, please forgive our selfishness and our frequent thoughts about quitting. Do grant us, however, your peace and rest. In Jesus' name we pray. Amen."

Winter

Scripture: "He came to what was his own, and his own people did not accept him. But to all who received him, who believed in his name, he gave power to become children of God" (John 1:11-12).

Jesus comes to us and bids us come to him. He came to us at Bethlehem. He sought us out in our salvation experience. God comes to us and bids us come to God through God's Son. That's one of the reasons we worship God. Sunday, God will come to the worship experience. We will come. The created will worship the Creator. The redeemed will worship the Redeemer. God will seek the seekers. All of this is to be announced by music. All of these expressions will be lifted and acknowledged and deepened by music. The choir leads the way. The choir can express, through music, the congregation's deep prayers of confession and repentance.

It is possible, however, to stand in the middle of the awesome intersection just described and miss the whole thing. Sometimes, the expectation level is very low. We hope that God has "tuned in" and is accepting what we're offering, but God's actual presence? We're not so sure. "He came to what was his own, and his own people did not accept him." The scene is tragic. We are reminded of Jacob's dream at Bethel: "Then Jacob woke from his sleep and said, 'surely the LORD is in this place—and I did not know it!' And he was afraid, and said, 'How awesome is this place! This is none other than the house of God, and this is the gate of heaven.' "(Gen. 28:16-17).

Jesus comes to his own in the house of God, the house of worship and no one knows it. He is not rejected; his presence is overlooked in the midst of worship.

The choir is not a group of above-average singers with a steady gig. The choir is a group of God-gifted and God-called ministers. Know he is present. Sing in awe of his presence. The congregation will catch on. And "to all who received him, he gave power to become children of God." How's that for a response to your singing? It beats applause anytime.

Prayer: "Dear God, help us always to be aware of your actual presence with us. Help that awareness inform and influence our singing and worship leadership. We pray this in the name of the One who sits beside us and resides within us. Amen."

Week 40

Hymn: *"Now Thank We All Our God," stanza 1:* *"Now thank we all our God, with heart and hands and voices, who wondrous things has done, in whom this world rejoices," words by Martin Rinkart.*

The concept of thanksgiving is not to be trifled with. Thankfulness is the first sign and expression that a person knows his or her relationship to the Creator. It's good that our nation takes a day off called "Thanksgiving." It's doubtful that the idea of being thankful would ever enter the minds of many people without the focus of the holiday. Furthermore, Thanksgiving ushers in the holiday season. Thankfulness followed by a season of celebrations seems appropriate.

Thankfulness followed by a season of celebration is also a good description of worship.

Even our hardened and hurried society expects a "thank you." Thankfulness as a way of life is something that is not as much at home in our society. It is something the church understands and rehearses each week. Perhaps the church should do more to disperse its concept of thanksgiving into the world.

When hearts and voices are rehearsed and focused on God's call and work, our hands become involved. We live our thankfulness. Living in a context of thankfulness will naturally affect how we approach the music our choir is to sing.

The world does rejoice in the gifts and beauty of God. Nonbelievers see rainbows. Nonbelievers are healed by modern medical miracles. The rain makes their gardens grow just as it does ours. But they are similar to us in another way: taking God's gifts for granted. We need to be reminded, the nonbeliever needs to be awakened to the fact that the God in whom we live and breathe is Love.

As an act of thankfulness, let us sing ourselves, our church, and our community into an awareness of the One "who wondrous things has done, in whom this world rejoices."

Prayer: "Dear God, thank you. Thank you for life and purpose and family and friendship. Forgive us when we take your gifts for granted. In Jesus' name. Amen."

Week 41 **Scripture:** *"Do not fear, for I am with you, do not be afraid, for I am your God; I will strengthen you, I will help you, I will uphold you with my victorious right hand" (Isa. 41:10).*

It is a sad and ironic fact that the holiday season is a fearful and depressing time for many people. In many parts of our country, the shorter days of winter are also the darkest and cloudiest of the year. Many people will overload credit cards. For others, wounds of broken families will be torn open by the "family holidays."

How are we to sing light and joy into dark and sad hearts that may venture into the sanctuary or into the choir loft? Perhaps we can begin by remembering that Advent is a time of acknowledging the darkness that surrounds us. We look forward to the light, but we do so in darkness. If our songs can point that out, the fearful ones will not feel so out of place. If we will look closely and listen carefully we can detect in our verse a hint of light beginning to glow just on the edge of the horizon of hope. The first three words of Isaiah 41:10 are "do not fear." That sounds like angels. That sounds like the angels reassuring the shepherds who are trying to make a living in the middle of the night; trying to make their way through the dark.

Let the congregation know the light in the distance is real and it's heading their way. Let the darkness know its nights are numbered. Let the fearful ones know they need not fear. God is with them and Jesus is coming to illuminate that fact. "I will strengthen you, I will help you, I will uphold you."

We need not tremble in the darkness. Let the darkness tremble in our hope. In *pianissimo* whispers, sing into the night: "Do not fear." It is a prelude to the anthem of the angels. We know that, but wait for the fullness of time. When the "Glorias" come, let them come in bright contrast to the full night we have endured.

Prayer: *"Dear God, thank you for your presence, even in our dark night. Thank you for Jesus, the Light of the World. We pray for those who are lonely and depressed during the holiday season. Help us to plant the hope of Advent in their hearts. Amen."*

Week 42

Scripture: "He will rejoice over you with gladness, he will renew you in his love; he will exult over you with loud singing as on a day of festival" (Zeph. 3:17).

We finally get old enough to understand why our parents enjoyed Thanksgiving as much as Christmas. Furthermore, we come to know that they really were happy to get socks as a gift. They were delighting in warm experiences of family love and in their children's joy.

Evidently, this is also true of our heavenly Parent. What an astounding scene! God singing and rejoicing over us as if at a holiday. This is especially intriguing to those of us who sing. No stern old man with a long gray beard here. This is not a picture of an angry deity just looking for a chance to zap lowly creatures that step out of line. Here is a happy God exulting and singing, having a party. And we seem to be the reason for the celebrating.

Does the God in this verse not know about our sinning? God knows who we really are yet rejoices over us and breaks out into singing. It is a reason to be obedient. It is reason enough to enjoy life—even life's little things. It is reason enough to be happy in the holiday season and to sing our happiness into the hearts of those who listen. It is reason to worship God in refreshing ways and with, perhaps, happier hearts. God knows us and rejoices. Let's join the party. Feasts and parties, bells and garland; it all seems appropriate in the scene described by our scripture verse.

Choir rehearsal is now preparation for a party. Thankfulness is the order of the day. "Family" is the environment. Celebration arches over our lives and worship—celebration that started in heaven.

Throughout the year, we have considered and committed to the choir's responsibility to be ministers. It is a formidable task. During this time of year (even with extra rehearsals and performances) let's remember that God is rejoicing, even singing over us. Let's join the song.

Prayer: "Dear God, thank you for the wonderful verse of scripture we have just read. Thank you for the love and grace that allows you to know us and yet rejoice over us. Help us as we endeavor to extend the party here on earth. In Jesus' name. Amen."

Week 43

Scripture: "Bless the LORD, O my soul, and all that is within me, bless his holy name" (Ps. 103:1).

"And all that is within me, bless his holy name." Praise and blessing seeping and soaking down into my inmost being—all that is within me. Praise can only intensify as it moves to the pressures at that depth; all that is within me, my inmost being. The darkness and the hardness that would inhabit and affect that space cannot resist God's light and forgiveness. Oh my soul, all that is within me, praise God's holy name. Do you know what else exists down at that level in our souls? Our music. We are coming nearest to the full realization of our call and task as worship leaders when we allow the music we sing to be the expression of our deepest selves. When our music comes from the depth of our soul, it targets the heart of God and the souls of those in the congregation. Worship takes place and it is life changing for every human being involved.

Praising God and blessing God's holy name become more than another subject or category of anthem texts. They move from being one of many options to being foundational to everything we do, say, and sing as a choir. When we allow praise and blessing first place in the choir's work and ministry, they will follow us home and to work. Through us and those in the congregation who "catch on," the entire church will become more aware of the place and importance of praise and blessing. "All that is within me" will begin to be applicable on a church-wide scale.

Great messages of truth can be dispersed, even launched, from the choir loft. Much of it will be carried on the wings of song, but not all. Much of it will also be carried in the person of the choir member. It will be delivered in personal relationships with members of the congregation and in work other than choir throughout the life and ministry of the church. "All that is within me" will not allow our praise and blessing to be confined to times when we are wearing choir robes.

The music in your choir folder is a sacred trust. So, too, the thoughts and focus of your soul. "Bless the Lord, O my soul, and all that is within me, bless his holy name."

Prayer: "Dear God, we pause to praise you and to bless your holy name. Help us to do so with the entirety of our being, the depth of our soul, and our music. In Jesus' name we pray. Amen."

Week 44

Scripture: *"A great windstorm arose, and the waves beat into the boat, so that the boat was already being swamped. But he was in the stern, asleep on the cushion; and they woke him up and said to him, 'Teacher, do you not care that we are perishing?' He woke up and rebuked the wind, and said to the sea, 'Peace! Be still!' Then the wind ceased, and there was a dead calm. He said to them, 'Why are you afraid? Have you still no faith?'"* *(Mark 4:37-40).*

Jesus could have calmed the storm at any time. But the storm did not concern him. The fear in the hearts of his disciples, however, did concern him. He calmed the storm to bring peace to the disciples' hearts. Perhaps it is still true. With Jesus' love flowing through us, we are to seek a calming of the souls around us as well. Nothing quite soothes the soul like music. How much more then, music that carries the words of God's presence and calming peace?

Jesus addressed the real storm before he went back to sleep. "Why are you afraid?" he asked them, "Have you still no faith?" Do storms of doubt still blow up suddenly within you? It's as if Jesus took care of the easy stuff first. He spoke to the frightening environment and it immediately calmed down. The harder task was to bring the disciples around to seeing things as Jesus saw them. The disciples still didn't get it. Rather than asking one another, "Who is this who can bring peace to our souls?" they asked, "Who then is this, that even the wind and the sea obey him?"

We often ask the wrong questions in the context of choir. "Why this piece of music?" "Why this well-worn 'war horse' again?" "Why did he/she get the solo?" "Why do we have to practice that section again?" There is another question, one worth waking the Master. It is, "What can I learn from this anthem at this time?"

Perhaps now is a good time to remind ourselves of an important fact. Now that Jesus is with us in spirit, no longer in a physical body, he never sleeps. He knows the severity of the storm clouds before we feel the first breeze. We are to pray, but not in order to inform Jesus of the storm. He knows. Admit being tossed around by the storm. Admit fear and feelings of helplessness. But pray acknowledging God to be the giver of peace and strength, not the handyman who remodels life to be the way we want it.

Prayer: "Dear God, bring peace and calm to our souls. Help us to model our desires and concerns after those of your Son, Jesus. Make us instruments of your peace. We pray this in Jesus' name. Amen."

Week 45

Hymn: "For All the Saints," stanza 1: "For all the saints, who from their labors rest, who thee by faith before the world confessed, thy name, O Jesus, be forever blest," words by William W. How.

Honoring those who have gone before us is good for the soul. It helps define who we are and what we are about. It lets us know that the things we accomplish are the results of team efforts, even though many team members have gone on to heaven. Whatever our choir will be in the future, it will be built on what our choir is now. Such awareness keeps us from approaching choir haphazardly. We have been entrusted with a call and with a heritage.

As you think back to some of the great names in the history of your choir, it may well be that their music is not what first comes to mind. Their heart and personality, their "presence" and spirit seem more important at this juncture.

The harmonization of the lives and friendships within the choir is so important. It honors the memory of those in the past. Such spiritual and emotional harmony recognizes the present as being important to the future. We thank Jesus for all the saints who from their labors rest, those who have gone on and those who are simply, in this rehearsal, resting a bit from the labors of the week.

It is Christlike to build a community, a family of caring and encouragement. That is what it means to honor the singing saints of the past. That is what future choir members need as a foundation for what they will build. Don't just leave them music to sing. Leave them the now-enhanced heritage that you received. Choir is a physical action, it is a musical endeavor, it is a spiritual act, and it is also an exercise in community. The words *ensemble* and *harmony* reinforce the concept. To speak of brothers and sisters in Christ and in choir is to define a family created by the Spirit and God's gifting.

Music is a gift, but so is the brother or sister who sits on either side of you. "For all the saints, who from their labors rest . . . O Jesus, be forever blest."

Prayer: "Dear God, thank you for my sisters and brothers in Christ. Thank you for these who share the gift of music. Thank you, also, for the saints who have gone on before. As a grateful recipient of their dedication, let me invest in the future by being obedient to the example of your Son, Jesus. It is in his name we pray. Amen."

Week 46

Hymn: *"We've a Story to Tell to the Nations,"* stanza 2: *"We've a song to be sung to the nations, that shall lift their hearts to the Lord, a song that shall conquer evil and shatter the spear and sword,"* words by H. Ernest Nichol.

This is the time of year when mission endeavors are spotlighted. Generosity stretches from the under the overpasses of our city to mission points around the globe. This is good and appropriate. We have grown to see missions in terms of agriculture, medicine, and engineering as well as church planting and evangelism. A genuine love for the people as well as a genuine love for the Good News of Jesus motivates us.

Such investment of love and self, of time and money can lead to the shattering of spears and swords. In the past spears and swords have been used to force the gospel on people. Even now, the spear and sword is sometimes used to "defend" against the gospel. Christ-followers help bring about the shattering of spears and swords.

Sharp words, steely glances, and hearts of stone are sophisticated weapons. They are the spears and swords of many battle-hardened Christians. Our songs are to shatter the spear and sword, wherever they are found. A soldier can win peace by silencing the enemy. The soldier will need, however, to keep a few spears and swords on hand, just in case. A humble Christ-follower with the heart of a servant can plant peace, using swords that have been retooled into plows. Christian soldiers are servants, singing the song that shatters the spear and sword.

Our song is to be sung to the nations. The nations are coming to us. People who used to be out of our reach are now just a few steps or a few keystrokes away. Some will be in the pews on Sunday. As different cultures increasingly share neighborhoods, schools, work-stations, and pews, we encounter new definitions of the word *nation*. In scripture, believers in Jesus are referred to as a "holy nation." We are set apart from those who do not claim Jesus as Savior. Such separation can lead to the use of spear and sword—real ones or the more sophisticated ones mentioned earlier. We've a song to be sung to the nations, that shall lift their hearts to the Lord, conquer evil, and shatter the spear and sword.

Prayer: "Dear God, help us to be agents of your peace. Peace on earth must be peace in hearts. In this season, especially, use us and our songs to shatter the spear and sword. In Jesus' name. Amen."

Week 47 *Hymn:* *"O Love That Wilt Not Let Me Go," stanza 3: "I trace the rainbow through the rain, and feel the promise is not vain, that morn shall tearless be," words by George Matheson.*

Even when some or most of the individual choir members don't feel like it, the choir is often called upon to "trace the rainbow through the rain." It's part of being ministers. You are ministers through music. During those times when tracing the rainbow is needed, just singing "Over the Rainbow" won't help.

The congregation sits in a downpour every Sunday morning. Even those who are enjoying happy times in their lives may well be sitting next to a person who is in a downpour of personal crises and hardships. The choir is called upon to trace the rainbow through the rain, to sing God's promises out into the storm.

This cannot be faked or manufactured. If you are in a time of great peace and happiness, report the existence of happiness through your singing. If you are one of those who is suffering privately and silently, sing from your own need and hope. You could have singers representing both life situations in a duet. Surely both are represented in a choir. Sing of the rainbow. Trace its outline for the congregation. Sing of the rainbow, but sing honestly. Honest tears are better than fake smiles, even while standing in the choir loft.

What is first and foremost an act of worship widens and deepens into ministry. Stand tall in the choir loft and through your music point to the rainbow.

The particular promise in our hymn says that the morning will be tearless. That could well be true literally. Spiritually, it is based on the promise in the psalm that though we may be experiencing a dark night of sorrow, joy comes in the morning.

Perhaps in this rehearsal, you need to let the words of the anthems trace the rainbow for you. A choir, like any other community of Christ-followers, is a company of wounded healers.

Stand in the choir loft and point to the rainbow that you have come to know so well.

Prayer: "Dear God, thank you for the gift of joy that penetrates our pain. Thank you for the rainbow promise of your presence and love for us. Strengthen us to honestly point to the rainbow. We pray this in Jesus' name. Amen."

Week 48

Scripture: *"How can you believe when you accept glory from one another and do not seek the glory that comes from the one who alone is God?" (John 5:44).*

Singing in public is a tricky matter, even when you do so in a choir. Musicians and nonmusicians alike know the protocol and etiquette of musical performance. One performs their very best, the audience acknowledges that by means of applause, and the performer graciously responds to the applause with a bow. It is a polite exchange at worst. At best, it is an enthusiastic acclamation of the performer's innate talent and disciplined cultivation of that talent. It is an interplay of heroes and critics, of entertainment and accomplishment.

What happens when the performance takes place in church in the context of worship? The soloist and/or choir work very hard in rehearsal. Notes are chased until caught, words are carefully enunciated, pitch is honed, ears are trained toward balance and blend, precision is demanded. That is hard work, work that is often deeply appreciated by the congregation. Shouldn't one politely acknowledge performances in church?

The entire scene, when played out in church, is tempered by the focus of it all. The words *congregation* and *audience* are not interchangeable in the worship setting. We have learned that God is the audience, those in the congregation are the players, and the worship leaders are the prompters. Who then, should do the applauding and who should do the bowing? Answer: The congregation should bow before God who, in all God's glory, will say "well done" in appropriate ways. All the while, the worship leaders are being careful to stay discretely offstage. We play, then, to an audience of one. To perform for one another in the worship setting is to ignore God or reduce God's place of prominence.

We must be gracious in receiving compliments. It would be easy to be impolite or overly pious in our response to such compliments. Neither of those is Christlike. So what is our hedge against eliciting or even just accepting glory that should go to God?

It's a matter of the heart. Rehearsing the soul ensures a performance that is in proper perspective. Our intent and motivation must be an expression of worship as surely as the performance itself.

Prayer: "Dear God, thank you for the opportunities to sing your praise and bring glory to your name. Forgive me when I hold back a little of the glory for myself. Help my life to say, 'To God be the glory.' In Jesus' name I pray. Amen."

Week 49

Hymn: *"Praise the Lord Who Reigns Above,"* stanza 2: *"Celebrate the eternal God with harp and psaltery, timbrels soft and cymbals loud in this high praise agree; praise with every tuneful string; all the reach of heavenly art, all the powers of music bring, the music of the heart,"* words by Charles Wesley.

Has it happened yet? Has the music of your skill and practice unlocked the music of your heart? We've all had moments when the music of our heart has seeped out and been a part of a performance. But have you been able to access that music and use it in praise and worship of God? Anything less is handing God part of what we have gathered up. It stops short of offering God all we are. For some, that depth of heart may be foreign territory. Busy lives don't visit down there as a matter of course. Things that are buried down there are buried for a reason. Yet, the fact remains that we cannot open the door for the music of the heart to be released without risking the escape of other things compressed into that deep and out of the way place. God wants it all. God deserves it all. God has made provision for it all.

Often the music of harp, psaltery, timbrels, and cymbals are decoys and smoke screens. Often the music of our skill and practice is offered as a "good enough" gift; a gift that has value, but stops comfortably short of baring our soul and giving our all. Compartmentalized Christianity or "followship" allows for partial gifts and expressions. Full, open praise, offering one's entire being to God cannot hide or hold back even the dark things.

The word *celebrate* appears in this stanza and demands to be acknowledged as the first word. God knows all there is to know about us. God even knows the bits and pieces we have tucked away in the dark recesses. Still, knowing that, God welcomes us to the throne in prayer and praise. That's something to celebrate. It is grace in abundance.

The music of the soul, coaxed out by celebration, will be renewed and freshened by the cool breezes of the Holy Spirit. Some of the celebrating will be quiet and personal. Some of it will be loud and public, overflowing to those around you.

Prayer: "Dear God, you know the depths of our hearts. Forgive the arrogance that allows us to think we can hide anything from you. Help us to move toward full expressions of confession and praise. This we pray in Jesus' name. Amen."

Week 50

Scripture: *"While Peter was still thinking about the vision, the Spirit said to him, 'Look, three men are searching for you. Now get up, go down, and go with them without hesitation; for I have sent them'"* *(Acts 10:19-20).*

Do you sing toward a vision? When you stand to sing in the choir loft, do you sing toward what the message of the anthem means to you? Do you sing toward a vision of what the message could mean to others? It's good to sing on Sunday "still thinking about the vision" that came into focus during the rehearsals. If the soul was rehearsed along with the music, the vision will be present and dynamic.

To simply sing another anthem with a message that may or may not have anything to contribute to worship is to pay homage to a routine. It is a nonchalant handling of a holy moment. God gives talent and songs and worship opportunities. Our loving response will include faithful stewardship of the gifts. Peter was instructed by the Holy Spirit to "get up, go down and go with them without hesitation." We soon see why. The Holy Spirit was setting the whole thing up. The Holy Spirit had sent the three men. The vision had purpose. So, too, there is purpose in the vision that we receive as we rehearse the music. Expect to hear "Now get up out of the rehearsal room, go out to the choir loft and sing to them without hesitation; for I have sent them." Each Sunday we are in a situation organized and orchestrated by the Holy Spirit.

There are people in the congregation who love music and get as much or more from the choir anthem as they do from the pastor's homily. They are the ones who are especially looking for you. Will you sing to them from your vision? Working with the Holy Spirit in these events of divine appointment will enrich your entire life.

Choir members are about the Lord's work. God doesn't abandon us once we've got "the hang of it." God is with us through the person of the Holy Spirit. This is the source of our vision, our talent, our energy, our purpose, and our hope of meaningful ministry.

Prayer: "Dear God, thank you for the Holy Spirit. Thank you for purpose in our lives. Thank you for the direction, strength, and encouragement that we need to fulfill that purpose. Lead us in this rehearsal toward next Sunday's divine appointment. In Jesus' name. Amen."

Week 51

Scripture: "He set himself to seek God in the days of Zechariah, who instructed him in the fear of God; and as long as he sought the LORD, God made him prosper" (2 Chron. 26:5).

Our scripture passage is describing young King Uzziah. He was a successful and prosperous king and now we know why. He prospered as long as he sought the Lord.

How does a church choir know if it is successful and prosperous? Is a choir successful simply if it sings at the right time in the liturgy and does so with a minimum of mistakes? Is a choir prosperous if it is continually growing in numbers? Is a choir successful if it is regularly moving on to "better" or more difficult music?

Before we can know if a choir is successful we must know what its task or assignment is. If you look back over the years, you may surmise that the choir's assignment is to sing at the beginning of a worship service and just before the homily. If that's a valid assessment then a choir's success can be measured in terms of musical performance. That's easy. Musicians are good at critiquing performances. The only disruption comes at the point of differing opinions about what a choir should sound like. We get good at wading in and out of those debates. But there is a haunting notion in the choir member's heart—a notion that a musical measurement of success is not all there is to our work.

The choir encourages congregational participation in worship. We do this mainly through our own enthusiastic singing of the hymns. The choir adds to the proclamation of the Word. The choir is a ministry in which people can use their God-given musical talent. The choir lifts the faith expressions of the congregation in a musical language that is beyond the ability of most in the congregation. These are starting to sound like real and worthwhile reasons for the choir's existence.

The question remains: "How does a choir know if it is successful or prosperous?"

If we are allowing ourselves as individuals and as a choir to be instructed in the fear of God and if we are seeking the Lord, we are achieving the success we are meant to achieve. There's another option and, sadly, it's the rest of the story for our young King Uzziah: "But when he had become strong he grew proud, to his destruction" (2 Chron. 26:16).

Prayer: "Dear God, humble our hearts so that we remain learners and seekers. In Jesus' name. Amen."

Week 52   ***Hymn:*** *"O God, Our Help in Ages Past," stanza 1: "O God, our help in ages past, our hope for years to come, our shelter from the stormy blast, and our eternal home!" words by Isaac Watts.*

If you have been in choir for any length of time you've seen changes in the music of the church. You have felt that the word *contemporary* seems to continually chip away at music that was once solidly grounded in traditional harmony and form. Harmony must now either make a statement or dissipate into thin air. Melodies are short and annoyingly repetitive. Rhythms have become inaccessible obstacle courses. And it seems that almost any words will do for a text as long as the name "Jesus" is included now and then.

If the first paragraph is foreign to you, maybe this will sound more familiar. Our choir can't or won't sing anything that was written after 1940. The music would be more at home in a funeral parlor or a museum. Only insomniacs could benefit from the stuff we sing. "Boring" is too kind a word for our ancient repertoire. Why can't we sing something that has some life to it?

Actually, you are fortunate if your choir contains proponents for each of the above sentiments. That says that you have bridged from one generation to the next and you can do it again. New music styles come more quickly than the rapidly passing years. Will it all move faster and faster until it finally explodes in some kind of a stormy blast? Some are asking, "Will change *ever* come to our church and our choir?" They have concluded that the stormy blast already occurred and they were left permanently stunned.

As choir members concerned about our church's music, what hope do we have for the years to come? As our hymn suggests, our help is our hope. Our help in getting this far is our only hope to move in the right direction in the years to come. Our God is our help and hope.

Choir, you have a wonderful call. Take a breath and step into the new year. One of these days we will take our last breath and step into a new choir; the heavenly choir of the redeemed, a choir whose music will stun the angels.

Prayer: "Dear God, our help in ages past, our hope for years to come, be our shelter in the stormy blast and our eternal home. Help us to remember that this world is not our home. While we are passing through help us to be diligent in rehearsing the music and rehearsing the soul. In Jesus' name. Amen."

Special Days

Christmas

Hymn: "Who Is He in Yonder Stall," stanza 1: "Who is he in yonder stall at whose feet the shepherds fall? 'Tis the Lord, O wondrous story! 'Tis the Lord, the King of glory;" words by Benjamin R. Hanby.

There is no busier time for the choir than Christmas. Preparation for the extra performances and worship events adds to the rush of the season. Garlands become nothing more than props that must be quickly and properly placed. Costumes help us pretend that we are someone else for a performance or two. Candles and candy, parties and presents, a year's dose of Christmas carols in the space of a few short weeks; it's a warm and mostly happy kind of chaos. Live animals and dead microphones compete with banners and bows for our time and creativity. And, oh yes, the manger—a doll this year or a real baby? Who is that in yonder stall?

The smallest participant in the pageant, lying in the roughest of the props, is the center of the whole frenzied celebration. Even in the center, the Christ child can be ignored. Musicians, don't let this happen to you or to your music. Don't let it happen to your church. Keep asking who is in the manger. Ask, too, who is in the music. If the Christmas music is just a part of your seasonal pressure, the question is all the more important in the midst of the greater rush.

There is a baby in the center of it all. The almighty God lies helpless as a baby because of God's love for us. If Mary doesn't care for him, he'll be run over by the Bethlehem crowd. Just like Mary, we must care for Jesus in the midst of the rush or he'll be run over or passed by. There's a baby in yonder stall, reminding us that we must become as children in order to enter the kingdom. Who is that in yonder stall? It is Jesus, reminding us that Christ is to be found among the poor and powerless. There's a baby in yonder stall reminding us of the power of humility.

Rehearsing the soul for this season will mean listening to the baby's cry in the Gospels and in your heart intently enough to be able to recognize it in the midst of all the holiday noise. The baby's cry is the birth of salvation. It is light breaking into darkness.

Prayer: "Dear God, bring your peace to my heart this Christmas. Renew the warmth of the season in my life. In Jesus' name. Amen."

Easter

Hymn: *"Ask Ye What Great Thing I Know,"* stanza 4: *"This is that great thing I know; this delights and stirs me so: faith in him who died to save, him who triumphed o'er the grave: Jesus Christ the crucified,"* words by Johann C. Schwedler.

There's all the difference in the world between sight-reading and singing a song you know. In fact, sight-reading is a proficiency in most music schools. One cannot graduate until this proficiency is mastered. We rehearse a piece of music many times in order to move it from "don't know" to "do know." When we stand in the choir loft, we are expected to know the anthem we're singing. In musical terms this is so foundational it seems silly to even mention it. Spiritually, however, this "knowing" cannot be taken for granted.

We would never think of sight-reading a piece in worship. Yet, it is possible to polish the enunciation, unify the vowels, and properly place the consonants without "knowing" the text. Learning the message of the text is part of rehearsing the soul.

On Easter Sunday, it is a glorious thing to stand and proclaim through music, "These things I know." It adds credence to the message of the anthem. It encourages the congregation. It is a statement of faith that strengthens the soul. "These things I know," our singing declares, "Jesus Christ defeats my fiercest foes, he consoles my saddest woes, he revives my fainting heart, he died to save." To sing such a testimony is to worship from the depths of one's experience, joy, and hope. Easter is the height of such joy and assurance. We are not sight-reading the text or passing along someone else's message. We are baring our soul and exposing our faith in great confidence and celebration. Christ is risen! He is risen, indeed! Ask ye what great thing I know? This is it, and I sing it boldly.

Such joy and confidence need not be confined to Easter Sunday. We are resurrection people. Each sunrise is a reminder of God's forgiveness, of God's faith in us. The Christian is never without hope, for even death has been conquered. Each Sunday, sing as if it were Easter Sunday and folks in the congregation may begin to believe that what they are hearing from the pulpit and choir loft just might be true.

Prayer: "Dear God, thank you for the resurrection of your son, Jesus. Thank you for the hope and joy of Easter. In Jesus' name. Amen."

Good Friday

Hymn: *"O Sacred Head, Now Wounded," stanza 3: "What language shall I borrow to thank thee, dearest friend, for this thy dying sorrow, thy pity without end?"* anonymous Latin, translated by Paul Gerhardt.

It seems fitting that an anonymous person asked one of Christianity's most profound questions. The question comes from the hearts of all of us. The vision of Jesus hanging on the cross bows our heads and sends pangs of imagined pain rushing to our hands and feet. Our sin darkens the whole scene, leaving what light there is focused on us, on me. Each drop of blood is accusing, naming my sin and me. Yet, Jesus only has words of forgiveness. The only one who ever lived a perfect life is suffering because of my selfishness, disobedience, and greed. The one who loves is being tortured because of my hate.

What language shall we borrow to say, "thank you"? Our native tongue, the language of humanity, has no words strong enough to bear the burden, deep enough to bear the emotion. We turn to music. We turn also to the promise that the Holy Spirit utters for us the prayers that are from our hearts, but beyond our words.

The congregation shares our dilemma. We minister to them as our music expresses their emotions. We need the strengthening presence of the Holy Spirit to be able to express our love and sorrow as well as that of the congregation. Our music will bend under the weight. Only prayer will shore it up. This must surely be why God placed minor keys into our musical structure. Our sin created the scene. Our music must help us interpret it.

Choir, lead the congregation reverently to the cross, one painful step at a time. Do nothing to lighten the load. Feel the full weight of the cross. But help the congregation to remember that Jesus' love and forgiveness change the sentence from "He died *because* of me" to "He died *for* me." Our language sags under the weight of gratitude, just as it sagged under the weight of guilt. What language shall we borrow?

Silence, more now than ever, becomes part of the music that is our borrowed language. When the music has finished its attempt to be our borrowed language, only silence remains; the purest of all languages.

Prayer: Sing all three stanzas of the hymn softly and *a cappella*.

Pentecost

Hymn: "Breathe on Me, Breath of God," stanza 3: "Breathe on me, Breath of God, till I am wholly thine, till all this earthly part of me glows with thy fire divine," words by Edwin Hatch.

The choir is seen more than heard. The music must be prepared toward the very best presentation possible. It is your responsibility. But if the choir is seen more than heard, we must pay some attention to what we look like. Our hymn suggests we might glow with God's fire. Sounds like a good way for what is seen and what is heard to complement each other. There is only one way for that to happen honestly. The Holy Spirit, who lives in the heart of each Christian, must be allowed to be seen through us.

Touched by the Holy Spirit, our anthem will be heard in each individual's heart-language. Our lives and our countenances will glow. Our worship will be authentic and the church will be energized. The breath of God is a reference to the Holy Spirit. Life breathed into Adam, then later into the church at Pentecost can be breathed into our church. It can be breathed into our lives. It can be breathed into our music. Music doesn't have to be louder and faster if the Holy Spirit energizes it. Our robes don't need sequins if our faces glow with God's fire. We don't have to change into our "church modes" if we are wholly God's.

What if our imaginations could envision the Holy Spirit enlivening our church? What if that renewal started in the choir? What if Pentecost started in my heart and then spread in these ways? The soul must be rehearsed toward readiness for that possibility. The Holy Spirit is in our hearts, but Pentecost must be our desire if the choir is going to be the first point of renewal.

Choir, sing with the breath of God. Watch fire ignite in the eyes of worshipers. Watch as your church goes out into its everyday world speaking the good news in the tongues of men and of angels; the language of the church translated into the language of the world. Choir, sing, so that the church will be moved by the Holy Spirit to speak.

Prayer: "Dear God, help our lives to burn with the presence of your Holy Spirit. In Jesus' name. Amen."

Index of Scripture

Index of Hymns